B-29 SUPERFORTRESS vs Ki-44 "TOJO"
Pacific Theater 1944–45

DONALD NIJBOER

Osprey Publishing
c/o Bloomsbury Publishing Plc
PO Box 883, Oxford, OX1 9PL, UK
Or
c/o Bloomsbury Publishing Inc.
1385 Broadway, 5th Floor, New York, NY 10018, USA
E-mail: info@ospreypublishing.com

www.ospreypublishing.com

OSPREY is a trademark of Osprey Publishing Ltd, a division of Bloomsbury Publishing Plc.

First published in Great Britain in 2017

© 2017 Osprey Publishing Ltd

All rights reserved. No part of this publication may be used or reproduced in any form without prior written permission except in the case of brief quotations embodied in critical articles and reviews. Enquiries should be addressed to the Publishers.

A CIP catalogue record for this book is available from the British Library

ISBN: PB: 978 1 4728 1886 7
        ePub: 978 1 4728 1888 1
        ePDF: 978 1 4728 1887 4
        XML: 978 1 4728 2192 8

17 18 19 20 21   10 9 8 7 6 5 4 3 2 1

Edited by Tony Holmes
Cover artwork and battlescene by Gareth Hector
Three-views, cockpits, armament scrap views and Engaging the Enemy artwork by Jim Laurier
Index by Alan Rutter
Typeset in ITC Conduit and Adobe Garamond
Maps and formation diagrams by Bounford.com
Page layouts by PDQ Digital Media Solutions, Bungay, UK
Printed in Hong Kong through World Print Ltd.

The images on pages 49 (bottom), 55, 56, 58, 59 (bottom), and 62 were originally published in AEU 5: *B-29 Hunters of the JAAF*, and that on page 54 in ACE 100: *Ki-44 'Tojo' Aces of World War 2*. Henry Sakaida kindly granted us permission to re-use these images. Every reasonable effort has been made to trace copyright holders of material reproduced in this book, but if any have been inadvertently overlooked the Publishers would be glad to hear from them.

Osprey Publishing supports the Woodland Trust, the UK's leading woodland conservation charity. Between 2014 and 2018 our donations are being spent on their Centenary Woods project in the UK.

To find out more about our authors and books visit **www.ospreypublishing.com**. Here you will find extracts, author interviews, details of forthcoming events and the option to sign up for our newsletter.

B-29 Superfortress Cover Art
On December 3, 1944 XXI Bomber Command sortied 86 B-29s on a large-scale attack on the Nakajima aircraft plant at Musashino, in western Tokyo. Seventy-six of the 73rd BW aircraft made it to the target area, where they dropped their bombs between 16,000 and 32,000ft. The Japanese fighter response was robust, with Ki-61 fighters from the 18th and 244th Hikō Sentai, Ki-45s from the 53rd Hikō Sentai, and Ki-44s from the 47th and 70th Hikō Sentai being scrambled. Northwest of Tokyo a formation of eight B-29s came under attack from an identical number of Ki-44s from the 47th Hikō Sentai, whose pilots introduced a new tactic when engaging the bombers. In coordinated attacks, a four-ship section would target a single B-29, with two Ki-44s diving head-on while the other two approached from astern. The pair in front tried to place their rounds into the cockpit area, while the Ki-44 pilots attacking from the rear aimed for the wing roots. Although no B-29s were shot down in this action by the Ki-44s, pilots from the 47th Hikō Sentai claimed five destroyed and seven damaged. Actual losses suffered by XXI Bomber Command amounted to five B-29s lost and 13 damaged. The bomber gunners in turn claimed ten confirmed victories, 11 probables, and 18 damaged – Japanese losses amounted to six fighters. (Cover artwork by Gareth Hector)

Ki-44 Cover Art
On November 24, 1944 the B-29s of XXI Bomber Command mounted the first daylight attack on Tokyo. A total of 175 Superfortresses hit targets in the docks and in urban areas, as well as the Nakajima aircraft plant in Musashino. Ki-44-IIs of the 47th Hikō Sentai caught the bombers over the target, with unit commander Maj Noburo Okuda raking B-29 42-24622 *Lucky Irish* of the 870th BS/497th BG, flown by 1Lt Sam Wagner, with 40mm cannon fire during a head-on attack. Moments later Cpl Yoshiso Mita finished the job by ramming his Ki-44 into the B-29's tail section. After he cut off the right stabilizer and elevator, his fighter burst into flames and fell from the sky. *Lucky Irish* went into a spin and eventually crashed nose first. There were no survivors. US losses amounted to two B-29s shot down and nine damaged, while the JAAF had five defending fighters destroyed.

Acknowledgements
I would like to thank Dominic Loucks, Nicholas Millman, Harvey Low, and Michael Mulligan for their assistance in the creation of this book.

CONTENTS

Introduction	4
Chronology	8
Design and Development	10
Technical Specifications	22
The Strategic Situation	33
The Combatants	39
Combat	52
Statistics and Analysis	71
Aftermath	75
Further Reading	78
Index	80

INTRODUCTION

"Every day our fighters went up to slash at the B-29s, and every day we achieved spectacularly little success."
Japanese ace Saburo Sakai

The Japanese knew the mighty B-29 was coming. Prior to its first flight Japanese intelligence had managed to gather a wealth of information on the new bomber, identifying some of the B-29's salient features. It had mid-mounted wings, four engines, and a total weight of 120,000lb (empty, the aircraft weighed 74,500lb). Bomb load was estimated at 20,000lb, with a defensive armament of ten or 12 0.50-cal machine guns and a single 20mm cannon. Astonishingly, the Japanese also concluded that the new B-29 would be pressurized as well, with an operational ceiling of close to 32,000ft and a top speed of almost 360mph. It was a remarkable assessment.

Their response to this highly accurate information was mystifying. Knowing what the Allies were prepared to do to win the war (the USAAF and RAF bombing campaign in Europe was well publicized), they did remarkably little to prepare a robust defense of the Home Islands. There was no crash program to modify existing fighters for high altitude flight. Like the majority of Japanese single-seat fighters, the Nakajima Ki-44 was equipped with a two-speed single stage supercharger. Japan's lack of two stage superchargers and the low displacement of its aircraft engines proved disastrous. The appearance of the B-29 forced the Japanese to develop fighters equipped with a turbo

B-29 42-24494 *MARY ANN* of the 792nd BS/468th BG releases its load of AN-M64 500lb high-explosive bombs on Hatto, Formosa, on October 18, 1944. The AN-M64 was the standard general purpose (GP) bomb carried by the B-29, with between 50 and 55 percent of the weapon's weight being high explosive. *MARY ANN* overshot the runway on June 17, 1945 and was written off. (National Museum of the USAF)

supercharger. The Nakajima Ki-87 and Tachikawa Ki-94, designed from the outset to intercept the B-29, appeared far too late. The Ki-87 failed to enter production and the Ki-94 never flew.

Fighter armament also remained worryingly light. The most numerous Japanese Army Air Force (JAAF) single-engined fighter, the Nakajima Ki-43-II, was armed with just two Ho-103 Type 1 12.7mm machine guns. This weapon was very similar in design to the classic Browning M-2 0.50-cal machine gun. Early experience with the rugged and well-armed and armored B-17 Flying Fortress and B-24 Liberator showed just how difficult they were to shoot down. Initial armament for the Ki-44-Ia was two Type 89 7.7mm and two Ho-103 12.7mm machine guns. What was needed was a well-armed fighter (fitted with at least four 20mm cannon) capable of high-altitude flight.

At the time of its introduction, the Boeing B-29 Superfortress was a truly awe-inspiring sight. Streamlined and powerful, it was an aircraft of purposeful design and inspiration. With a wingspan of 141ft and length of 99ft, the aircraft was considerably larger than its predecessor, the B-17. It would also be the most expensive weapons system developed during the war, costing in excess of $3 billion, which was about $1 billion more than the atomic bomb project. Finally, it was a bomber of many firsts. The world's first to be fully pressurized, the B-29 was powered by the largest piston engines built during the war. It also boasted the most advanced computer-aided remote controlled turret fire control system in existence.

In September 1942, when the first B-29 took to the air, the Nakajima Ki-44 Shoki attained limited production, with 40 Ki-44-Is and 83 Ki-44-IIs produced by the end of that year. Most were assigned to homeland defense squadrons and the Akeno Army Flying School. The Ki-44 represented a major departure from earlier Japanese fighter designs. Running almost in parallel with the Nakajima Type 1 single-seat "light" fighter, which became the Ki-43 Hayabusa, the Ki-44 was designed from the outset as a heavy fighter. Before war broke out both the JAAF and Imperial Japanese Naval Air Force (IJNAF) placed an emphasis on fighter agility and maneuverability. This design philosophy came at a price. While both of their principal fighters (the Ki-43 and the A6M2 Zero-sen) were extremely nimble, they carried no armor plate or self-sealing fuel tanks. Allied pilots quickly found that the Ki-43 and A6M2 caught fire after being hit by only a short burst of 0.50-cal machine gun fire.

Painted in the standard USAAF heavy bomber olive drab and grey camouflage of the period, 41-002 was the first of three XB-29s prototypes built by Boeing. Fitted with three-bladed propellers, the prototype lacked any turrets or tail guns. After initial taxi trials and a few brief test "hops," the aircraft's first proper flight took place on September 21, 1942. (National Museum of the USAF)

The Ki-44 would be different. Powered by a Nakajima Ha-41 engine developing 1,250hp, the new fighter was to have a maximum speed in excess of 372mph at 13,000ft, a range of 746 miles and the ability to reach 16,500ft in less than five minutes. Early armament consisted of two 7.7mm Type 89 and two 12.7mm Ho-103 machine guns. Equipped with pilot armor plate and self-sealing fuel tanks, it would prove to be one of the fastest climbing Japanese fighters of the war.

While well recognized as one of the most famous bombers of World War II, the B-29 did not emerge from the production line and into combat service without a long period of technical gestation. When the prototype XB-29 went aloft for the first time on September 21, 1942, very few imagined it would take another 21 months to make it close to combat ready. Technical problems with the Wright R-3350-23 Cyclone 18 twin row turbocharged radial piston engine would dog the B-29 until the end of the war. Indeed, more Superfortresses would be lost due to mechanical failure, malfunction, and reasons unknown than to enemy action. The R-3350 would prove to be the B-29's Achilles heel.

Overheating and engine fires were common. To save weight and improve performance the R-3350 was equipped with a magnesium crankcase. While very strong, it was, unfortunately, flammable, and once it caught fire it was almost impossible to put out. For B-29 crews, takeoff was the most critical phase, and the most frightening. An overloaded Superfortress required full power from all four engines. Nursing a fully loaded B-29 down a hot, humid runway required intense concentration by the flight engineer. If one engine caught fire, quit or dropped slightly in power the aircraft invariably crashed. Tail gunner Andy Doty of the 19th Bomb Group (BG) recalled, "Among the saddest sights to be seen by departing crews as they took off was the flaming wreckage of a bomber below them at the end of the runway." Consequently, early combat operations did not instill a great deal of confidence in the B-29. Many crews began to fear their own aircraft more than enemy fighters and flak.

The B-29's principal technological advancement centered on its ability to travel very far with a heavy bomb load. But it was its defensive armament that proved truly revolutionary, the bomber being fitted with four General Electric (GE) remote controlled turrets and a single tail turret. Using computerized gunsights, gunners were now capable of tracking incoming fighters with greater accuracy. All four turrets and the tail position were linked by five electromechanical computers that automatically corrected for ballistics, parallax, and lead position once the bullets arrived at their destination. They also allowed for one gunner to control multiple turrets at the same time. But, for all its promise, the new Central Fire Control (CFC) system could not keep the Japanese fighters at bay. Like the R-3350 engine, the CFC system would also be plagued by mechanical glitches and failures.

In December 1941 seven pre-production and two prototype Ki-44s were sent to China for combat evaluation. The pre-production models were capable of 374mph at 12,860ft, and they had an equally impressive rate of climb. During high speed trials the Ki-44 reached a top speed of 528mph in a dive without any adverse handling characteristics. For pilots accustomed to the more nimble Ki-27 and Ki-43, the new Ki-44 lacked good cockpit visibility, was nowhere near as maneuverable, and had a high landing speed. There were those, however, who appreciated its high diving speed,

A Ki-44-II Ko has its engine run up prior to making another flight with the JAAF's Air Test Department at Tama airfield, near the city of Fussa in western Tokyo. The three red vertical stripes that are just visible on the rear fuselage may indicate that this is the third Ki-44-II Ko delivered to the JAAF, which was the subject of extensive armament trails. (National Museum of the USAF)

excellent rate of climb, improved rate of roll, and heavier armament. As a result, the Koku Hombu (Imperial Japanese Army Air Headquarters) considered the Ki-44 suitable as an anti-bomber interceptor fighter and ordered limited production.

Combat operations for the B-29 began on June 5, 1944, when 98 examples from the 40th BG took off from their bases in India and headed for the Makasan railway depot near Bangkok. One crashed on takeoff due to an engine fire and 17 more would abort due to engine failure or other mechanical malfunctions. At the target a gathering undercast obscured the aiming point, resulting in little or no damage being inflicted on the depot. Five bombers crashed upon landing, with 42 more being forced to divert to other airfields because of a lack of fuel. The weather conditions and mechanical woes experienced during this first mission would go on to plague the B-29 force for the rest of the war.

The first B-29 to be shot down by Ki-44s fell on July 29. As 60 B-29s attacked the Showa steelworks at Anshan, in Manchuria, five Ki-44s from the 9th Hikō Sentai rose to intercept. After repeated attacks they managed to shoot down flak-damaged B-29 42-6274 *Lady Hamilton* of the 468th BG. The bomber's demise was credited to the sentai's newly appointed commanding officer, Maj Takehisa Yakuyama.

The high-altitude battles fought over Japan in 1944–45 would prove difficult for both B-29 gunners and Ki-44 pilots. Powerful jet stream winds hindered formation flying, forcing many bombers to fly as a single ship and not in a combat box formation. Flying above 27,000ft, Ki-44 pilots found their aircraft difficult to control – they often stalled out as they climbed. Desperate to inflict damage on the B-29, the Japanese formed special air-to-air ramming units called Shinten Seiku Tai (Heaven Shaking Air Superiority Units) of four aircraft each. When stripped of armament, armor, gunsight, and radios, the Ki-44 was thought to be capable of reaching 45,000ft. Unfortunately for the Superfortress crews, the Shoki-equipped ramming units were some of the most successful of the conflict over the Home Islands.

In the war against the B-29, the Ki-44 was one of the few Japanese single-seat fighters that was used as a bomber interceptor, ramming aircraft, and nightfighter, all with varying degrees of success.

CHRONOLOGY

1938
Summer US Army Air Corps (USAAC) Chief of Staff Maj Gen Oscar Westover establishes a requirement for a super bomber.

1939
June Work on the new Ki-44 begins. Emphasis is placed on high speed and fast rate of climb.

1940
August The first Ki-44 prototype (4401) begins flight-testing.

1941
September The Dokuritsu 47th Hikō Chutai (Independent 47th Air Squadron) is formed to evaluate the Ki-44 in combat. Seven pre-production and two Ki-44 prototypes are assigned to the 47th Hikō Chutai in Burma.

1942
January Forty Ki-44-Is are ordered into production, the aircraft being given the name Shoki (Demon).
September The Ki-44 is officially adopted by the JAAF as the Army Type 2 single-seat fighter Model I.
September 21 First flight of the XB-29 prototype.
December Only 40 limited-production Ki-44-Is and 83 mass-production Ki-44-IIs have left the Nakajima factory by year-end.

1943
January The 33rd Hikō Sentai becomes the first JAAF unit in China to receive the Ki-44, with five aircraft being delivered at the beginning of the year.
February 18 The second XB-29 prototype (41-003) crashes.
June 14 The first YB-29 service test aircraft takes flight (14 built, 41-36954 to 36967).
June 1 The 58th Bombardment Wing (Very Heavy) is activated at Marietta, Georgia.
July The first production B-29 is completed.
December The decision is made by the Allies not to use the B-29 against Germany.
December 31 Only 73 pilots are qualified to fly the B-29.

1944
January Only 97 B-29s have been built to date, with just 16 of them deemed to be airworthy at that point.
April Ki-44 production peaks, with 85 aircraft rolling off the production line that month.

A captured Ki-44-II Hei, coded S-11, in the hands of the Technical Air Intelligence Unit – Southwest Pacific. This aircraft was restored to flying condition and tested extensively against other Allied fighters including the P-51 Mustang, F6F Hellcat and, quite possibly, a Seafire III of the Royal Navy's Fleet Air Arm. (NARA)

April 2	The 58th BW reaches India with the first B-29s to deploy overseas.
April 4	The Twentieth Air Force is established to control XX and XXI Bomber Commands. It is the only numbered US air force created to operate a single type.
May	The Imperial Japanese Army launches the *Ichi-Go* ground offensive in China. One of its prime objectives is to "forestall the bombing of the Japanese homeland by American B-29s from bases in Kweilin and Liuchow."
June 5	The B-29 makes its combat debut, 98 examples flying from bases at Kharagpur and Makasan, in India, and heading for the Makasan railway depot in Bangkok. Seventy-seven reach the target. Six aircraft are lost to accidents and three ditch in the Bay of Bengal.
June 15	The US Marine Corps launches an amphibious invasion of Saipan, in the Mariana Islands archipelago. Guam and Tinian are attacked on July 21 and 23, respectively.
June 15/16	B-29s make their first bombing attack on Japan when 68 examples target the Yawata steel works on the Island of Kyushu. Seven are lost, only one of which is shot down by Japanese fighters.
July 7/8	18 Superfortresses flying from China encounter seven Ki-44 "Tojos" for the first time over Kyushu, with inconclusive results.
July 9	Saipan is officially secured, with more than 3,000 Marines having been killed during the invasion.
July 29	The first B-29 is shot down by Ki-44s, this aircraft being one of 60 targeting the Showa steelworks at Anshan, in Manchuria. The bomber falls to the 9th Hikō Sentai.
August 29	Maj Gen Curtiss E. LeMay takes command of XX Bomber Command.
October 12	The first B-29 arrives on Saipan.
October 28	XXI Bomber Command flies the first B-29 mission from Saipan when 18 bombers from the 73rd BW attack the submarine pens on Truk.
November 1	F-13 (B-29 reconnaissance variant) 42-93852 *TOKYO ROSE* of the 3rd Photographic Reconnaissance Squadron (PRS) flies over Tokyo. It is the first enemy aircraft to be seen over the Japanese capital since the "Doolittle Raiders" of April 1942. Ki-44-II Otsus are scrambled but are unable to reach the high-flying F-13.
November 24	The first successful ramming attack by a Ki-44 takes place over Tokyo, the aircraft of Cpl Yoshiso Mita of the 47th Hikō Sentai shearing off the elevator and horizontal stabilizer of a B-29 from the 497th BG, which crashes into the sea off Honshu.

1945

January	Ki-44 production comes to an end, with 1,223 examples having been built.
March 9/10	First fire-bombing raid on Tokyo takes place, 380 B-29s burning 16 square miles and killing an estimated 80,000 people. Two Ki-44-II Otsus armed with 40mm wing cannon of the 70th Hikō Sentai claim two B-29s shot down.
June 26	Ki-44s of the 246th Sentai record the last ramming attacks against the B-29. Three bombers are claimed for the loss of three pilots.
August 6	B-29 44-86292 *ENOLA GAY* of the 509th Composite Group (CG) drops the world's first atomic bomb on Hiroshima.
August 14	The longest, and last, B-29 mission of the war is flown when 143 B-29s from the 315th BW attack the Nippon Oil Company refinery at Akita, 275 miles northwest of Tokyo.

DESIGN AND DEVELOPMENT

"… we had the buggiest damn airplane that ever came down the pike."
Maj Gen Curtiss LeMay

BOEING B-29 SUPERFORTRESS

On the drawing board three years before the attack on Pearl Harbor and America's entry into the war, the B-29 would be the ultimate expression of the self-defending bomber and the centerpiece of the Allied strategic bombing campaign against Japan, ending with the world's first two atomic bomb attacks. Shaped from 27,000lb of sheet aluminum, the B-29 comprised 1,000lb of copper, 9.5 miles of wiring, two miles of tubing, and 600,000 rivets. It was a technological marvel that introduced a number of features that had never been seen or tried before. These included two computerized radar-directed bomb aiming systems (the AN/APQ-13 and AN/APQ-7 Eagle), the CFC system, individual dual bomb-bays, and heated and pressurized crew stations.

Its origins can be traced back to the years leading up to the outbreak of war in Europe, when senior staff officers within the USAAC had fully embraced the untested air power theories developed at its Tactical School at Maxwell Field, in Alabama. These theories centered on the high-altitude self-defending bomber and its ability to destroy enemy forces before they were deployed in the field and wreck any country's will to resist. It was in this context that the Boeing B-29 was born.

During the summer of 1938 USAAC Chief of Staff Maj Gen Oscar Westover established a requirement for a new super bomber. At the time the US aviation industry was well ahead of the rest of the world when it came to the design and construction of four-engined heavy bombers. Aircraft such as the Boeing XB-15 and Douglas XB-19 were prime examples, both designed with a range of 5,000 miles. In January 1940 the USAAC issued additional requirements in the form of request for Data R-40B. The new specification called for a pressurized bomber capable of speeds up to 400mph, with a maximum range of 5,333 miles and a bomb load of 2,000lb to be dropped at the halfway point. By March the USAAC had increased its demands with the issuing of Type Specification X-218-A, which called for a larger bomb load of 15,000–20,000lb, powered turrets, and a service ceiling of 30,000–40,000ft.

The clean aerodynamic lines of the B-29 are accentuated in this aerial view. Early examples were armed with ten 0.50-cal machine guns, with two weapons in the forward dorsal turret – this would later be changed to four. Although B-29 42-6242 would serve in the CBI theater, it would never drop any bombs. Permanently modified into a tanker, the aircraft was christened *Esso Express*. (National Museum of the USAF)

Boeing saw this as an opportunity. Confident in their ability, the company's management pressed ahead with a new super bomber design well before any government funds began to flow. On May 11, 1940, Boeing formally submitted its Model 345 design. Sufficiently interested, the USAAC awarded the company enough funds for additional studies and wind tunnel tests on June 17.

Consolidated, Lockheed, and Douglas also submitted designs, although the latter two companies would subsequently drop out of the competition. On August 24, 1940, funds for the construction of two XB-29 and two Consolidated XB-32 prototypes were released. On December 14 a third XB-29 static test airframe was also ordered.

By the fall of 1940, war with a rampant Germany was now seen as almost inevitable in the USA. The need for a new bomber was so pressing that the USAAC took the unprecedented step of ordering volume production of the B-29 *before* the first prototype took to the air, placing an order for 250 bombers on May 17, 1941. After the IJNAF's surprise attack on Pearl Harbor on December 7, 1941 and the US entry into the war that immediately followed in its wake, the contract was increased to 500. By March 1942, and with the prototype still six months away from making its first flight, that number had risen to 1,644 B-29s.

The first two XB-29s built by Boeing were equipped with four Wright R-3350-13 Cyclone radial air-cooled engines. Prototype 41-002 completed its first flight on September 21, 1942, with Boeing's Chief Test Pilot Edmund T. Allen at the controls. He reportedly expressed his doubts regarding the XB-29's complexity after this flight. On December 30, 1942 the second XB-29 (41-003) was forced to land with one engine in flames. The following day another Wright R-3350 sputtered and choked at 20,000ft. The problems continued. On February 17, 1943, a serious fuel leak forced another emergency landing.

The next day Allen and his crew would be the first of many to be killed by the unreliable and dangerous R-3350 when XB-29 41-003 suffered a serious engine fire that spread to the main spar. As the aircraft descended, flames tore into the left wing.

11

The B-29 was equipped with a revolutionary CFC system for its turrets. Using analog computers, it was set up so the upper gunner (and overall gunnery commander) controlled the upper aft turret, the left and right blister gunners operated the lower aft and forward turrets, the bombardier manned the forward upper turret, and the tail gunner controlled the rear turret. The genius of the system was that it allowed the individual gunners to override the system and assume control of one or more turrets when required. (Author's Collection)

The crew was unable to extinguish the fire and the XB-29 crashed into a Seattle meat-packing plant, killing 19 on the ground along with the entire 11-man crew. All aircraft using the R-3350 were grounded, pending an investigation led by Senator Harry S. Truman. The senate committee duly blamed the problems with the new B-29 program directly on the engine, leveling charges of poor workmanship and inspection. According to the report the USAAC was also equally to blame for putting too much pressure on Wright to accelerate R-3350 production. However, as frontline USAAF experience with the B-29 would graphically show, the problems with the engine ran much deeper than just shoddy workmanship performed by a rushed workforce. The R-3350 would prove to be notoriously unreliable and, in far too many cases, deadly.

A huge 18-cylinder air-cooled twin row radial, the R-3350 produced 2,200hp – by comparison, the B-17's four Wright R-1280-97 engines were rated at 1,200hp each. The twin-bank configuration of the R-3350 caused a series of cooling problems. Engine fires were the most serious of these, but runaway propellers or engines that simply disintegrated were common as well.

When engineers began work on creating the R-3350 in January 1936, their aim was to create an engine that produced one horsepower for each pound of weight. It was an overly ambitious target. To reduce weight Wright replaced the conventional aluminum-alloy crankcase and other accessory hosing with lighter magnesium-alloy parts. Under combat loads the brittle magnesium tended to crack under severe vibration. Magnesium also burned at an extremely high temperature. Once alight, an in-flight engine fire was virtually impossible to put out. Cylinder overheating also caused the lubricating oil to burn off the valves, resulting in them being "swallowed" and then causing an inevitable engine fire. Unfortunately, the B-29's on board extinguishers proved inadequate, unable to cope with 87 percent of reported fires. Amazingly, before the R-3350 finally entered service it would undergo 48,500 engineering and tooling changes.

The overriding key to the B-29's success lay with its streamlining. To attain its great speed, range, and ceiling, the design had to be as aerodynamically clean as possible. Every panel, vent or scoop was deleted or streamlined. All external rivets were flush and, more critically, the turret armament had to be streamlined as well. This meant that manned turrets were out of the question. Bendix, GE, Westinghouse, and Sperry all vied for the contract, with the latter company initially being chosen. The first three XB-29s were equipped with the Sperry system of retractable turrets and periscope gunsights, but when both proved to be unworkable, Boeing was forced to withdraw the contract and award it to GE.

The GE CFC system featured four streamlined, stationary, non-retractable turrets and a manned tail turret. All but the latter turret were operated by four remotely positioned gunners (one CFC gunner, two left and right blister gunners and the bombardier, who operated the front dorsal turret) using the first computerized gunsights. Equipped with five defensive turrets – upper forward, lower forward, upper rear, lower rear, and tail – early B-29s were armed with Browning M-2 0.50-cal machine guns in the four CFC turrets, while the tail position boasted an additional M-2 Type B 20mm cannon. The addition of the 20mm cannon, while boosting firepower, was not a good fit, for the ballistic properties of its shells were so different from the 0.50-cal bullets that there was no chance of a simultaneous hit on an incoming enemy fighter. The cannon was soon deleted, beginning with Boeing-Wichita production block 55, Bell-Atlanta block 25, and Martin-Omaha block 25.

A posed shot of a factory fresh B-29 showing the upper rear turret and blister position. This was the CFC gunnery commander's position, and with a 360-degree view, he was responsible for assigning the individual turrets to the other gunners when needed. Each gun was provided with 500 rounds of ammunition. (Author's Collection)

To provide greater protection against frontal attacks, the upper turret's armament was doubled to four guns. Unfortunately, trials showed the four-gun turret to have a greater bullet dispersal, resulting in the same number of hits as the previous two-gun version.

Like the R-3350 engine, the GE remote turret system only added to the B-29's complexity and mechanical setbacks. Originally, the USAAF had pushed for a manual system, hoping gunners would be able to solve the ballistic equations visually. It was a tall order, considering one gunner could have control of two turrets simultaneously. Aiming two turrets visually was impossible, which meant that all the geometric and ballistic calculations involved in accurately targeting an approaching enemy fighter would have to be done electromechanically by an analog computer.

The heart of the CFC system consisted of four 50lb electromechanical computers, each linked to a remote gunnery station. Unfortunately, the new analogue computers were rushed into production. Built by recently trained workers, new CFC systems installed in the first production B-29s were found to be in poor condition – installation problems would plague the system. Just prior to the first wing of B-29s heading to India, a crash program was instituted to bring the GE system up to an operational level. Although company reps worked 16- and 24-hour shifts correcting the mistakes made on the assembly line, even with the fixes the CFC system did not always work as advertised.

Crews seeing combat with the B-29 for the first time went into action in an aircraft that was dangerously unsafe. As one anonymous gunner said at the time, "Only those who readied this plane and flew it can fully know the harsh pains of its birth and dangerously rapid development, of explosive decompression at altitude, of engine

13

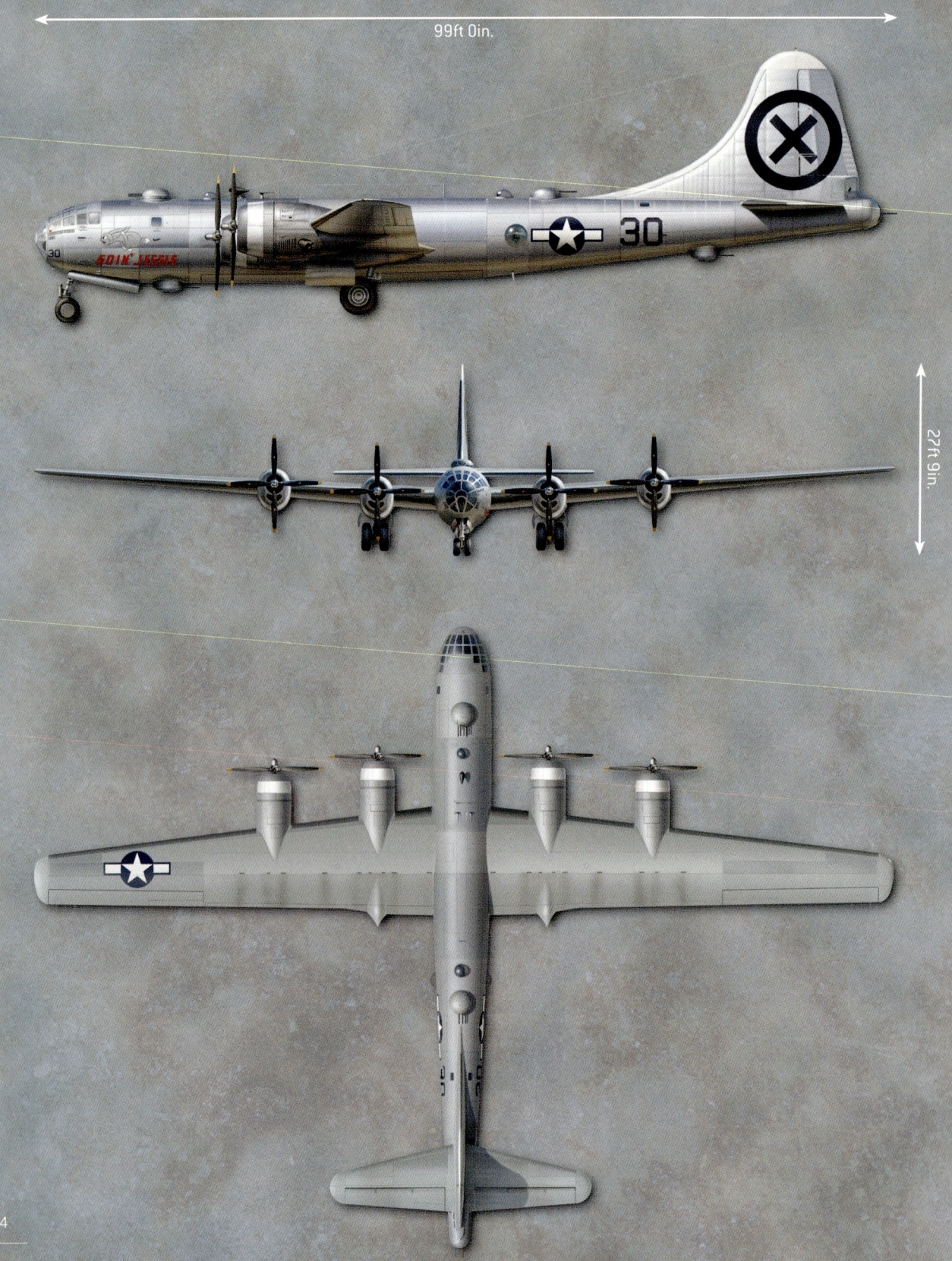

temperatures soaring above 300°C, of props that refused to feather, of remote controlled turrets 'cooking off' and spraying wildly." As the problems were worked out and gunners began to find their range, the new remote turret system did prove itself. Matched with the B-29's high-altitude performance, the CFC system was effective in combat, but ultimately it was not enough. Lightly armed Japanese fighters with limited high-altitude performance still managed to shoot down the high-flying B-29.

Ironically, for all the effort, expense, and ingenuity expended by GE, the B-29's defensive armament was removed once Maj Gen Curtiss LeMay switched to low-altitude night missions. Furthermore, introduction of the Bell-manufactured B-29B all but eliminated the turrets and fire control system except for the tail guns.

The Superfortress was a very good design, but significant shortcuts had been made in the race to get it into service. Defects and quality problems were so numerous that of the first 97 B-29s built by mid-January 1944, just 16 were airworthy. This was an embarrassing start to the aircraft's career with the USAAF, but there was no turning back. Up to this point the US Government had committed $1.5 billion to the project, and the USAAF needed its super bomber for three reasons – the defeat of Japan through strategic bombing, as an instrument to gain its independence from the US Army, and, most importantly, it needed an aircraft capable of dropping the atomic bomb that was then in development.

To get the massive project back on track, the USAAF exerted its control over Boeing. The "B-29 Special Project" was set up by Gen H. H. "Hap" Arnold, Commanding General of the USAAF, who, in late 1943, said, "It is my desire that this airplane be produced in quantity so that it can be used in this war and not in the next." In March 1944 Maj Gen Bennett Meyers, deputy to the Assistant Chief of Air Staff of the USAAF and future head of Materiel Command, was given full authority by Arnold to get all existing B-29s modified and combat ready. It was a herculean task. From all over America, USAAF groundcrews, technicians, and 600 workers pulled from the Wichita assembly line gathered at the Wichita plant and other USAAF Modification Centers.

Each B-29 was modified inside and out, with 75 aircraft needing new cockpit glass panels. Internally, every electrical plug had to be removed, disassembled, and re-soldered. All the R-3350-23s were removed and modified to R-3350-23A "war engine" specification, while undercarriage tires were replaced, radars fitted, and long-range fuel tanks installed in the bomb-bays. To make matters worse most of the work was done outside in frigid temperatures and frequent snow storms. After five exhausting weeks, the first "combat ready" B-29s started departing Wichita for airfields in the China-Burma-India (CBI) Theater of Operations. The "Battle of Kansas" had been, in many ways, a conditional victory. So urgent was the need for operational B-29s, shortcuts were taken. This meant that the Superfortress was heading for war as an immature weapons system. For Maj Gen Curtiss LeMay, the B-29's defects were all too obvious. "There were scores of other defects, either readily apparent or – worse – appearing when an aircraft was actually at work and at altitude."

With a paucity of serviceable B-29s, aircrew training suffered as well. When the 58th BW was established in the summer of 1943 it was short of everything, especially Superfortresses. Until more were made available, some squadrons had to train on Martin B-26 Marauder twin-engined medium bombers and older model B-17s.

OPPOSITE

B-29-50-BW 42-24856 *GOIN' JESSIE* of the 5th BS/9th BG, based at North Field, Tinian, in early 1945, was one of the few Superfortresses to complete 51 successive combat missions without an abort. During its tour the Superfortress delivered more than 330 tons of bombs, flew 700 combat hours, and covered more than 135,000 miles. It also happened to be the B-29 that dropped the 2,000,000th ton of bombs on Japan. *GOIN' JESSIE* is depicted here in the revised 9th BG markings, featuring the 313th BW circle containing the group letter "X" and the group color – white – on both the tail and engine nacelles. The previous fin markings had consisted of a small "X" above a black triangle, then the aircraft's serial and a black "9," all aligned vertically. Returning home to the USA on December 4, 1945, 42-24856 was scrapped in May 1954.

Unperturbed by the calamitous state of the B-29 program, and the fact that the first nuclear device would not be tested until July 1945, the USAAF was already making plans (from late 1943) for the Superfortress to fill the role of the world's first atomic bomber. Under the codename Project *Silverplate*, 36 B-29s were specially modified to carry two differently shaped bombs that would ultimately be dropped on the Japanese cities of Hiroshima and Nagasaki. The aircraft's twin bomb-bays were reconfigured to handle a single five-ton bomb that was up to 128 inches in length and as much as five feet in diameter.

The *Silverplate* bombers were just a tiny part of the massive B-29 orders placed by the USAAF with Boeing – orders which proved too large for the company to handle on its own. The contracts were eventually split between three companies, which would result in B-29s being built in four newly constructed, government-owned, aircraft assembly plants. All told, 2,749 B-29s were produced by Boeing, 531 by Glenn L. Martin, and 663 by the Bell Aircraft Corporation.

NAKAJIMA Ki-44 SHOKI

"A small compact aircraft that is a pronounced departure from previous Japanese design. Has an exceptional rate of climb and a high diving speed. One series was constructed with 40mm wing cannon." – *TAIC 155A Performance and Characteristics*

The primary mission of the JAAF fighter force was to establish air superiority over the battlefield. As a tactical force, its sole purpose was to provide support for the Imperial Japanese Army. Throughout the 1920s and 1930s Japanese single-seat fighter designs centered on extreme maneuverability. In many ways it was an obsession. The traditional dogfight of one-on-one combat with single enemy aircraft was a throwback to World War I. Many saw it as the raison d'être for all Japanese fighters, and, when combined with the Samurai tradition of single combat, it was a design philosophy that led directly to the Nakajima Ki-27 "Nate" and Ki-43 "Oscar." While both fighters adhered to the design philosophy of light weight, light armament, and agility, Nakajima was also working on a more innovative machine.

The 1930s was a decade of rapid transition. The introduction of the all-metal monoplane turned military aviation upside down. Aircraft like the Martin B-10 monoplane bomber, which entered service in November 1934, represented a quantum leap forward. In a single stroke all biplane fighters were rendered obsolete. Not only was the B-10 faster, it was of all-metal construction, had retractable landing gear, an enclosed bomb-bay and cockpit, variable pitch propellers, and a forward manual turret.

The increase in speed, durability, and defensive armament of the B-10 created a dilemma for fighter aircraft designers around the world. New monoplane fighters with more than two rifle-caliber machine guns resulted in aircraft that had a higher wing loading and were less maneuverable. For the Japanese the new monoplane designs like the British Hurricane and German Bf 109 represented a design paradox. These fighters were created from the outset to be pure interceptors, with good rates of climb, high speed, and heavy armament (the Hurricane was equipped with eight 0.303-in caliber machine guns). These new, powerful, fighters also required a revised set of combat tactics. Good maneuverability was now seen as a defensive asset rather than an attacking necessity.

While Japanese fighter design has always historically been defined by the nimble Ki-43 and A6M2 Zero-sen, and their early dominance in the Pacific, there was also a realization within both the JAAF and the IJNAF that a new interceptor influenced by European aircraft would be desirable. In 1936 the JAAF was offered an alternative. The Nakajima Hikoki KK (Nakajima Aircraft Company) developed an experimental new fighter known as the Ki-12. Created as a private venture, the Ki-12 was designed by Shigenobu Mori and was strongly influenced by the French Dewoitine D.510. The Ki-12 was an all-metal monoplane, with an open cockpit and retractable landing gear – a first for a Japanese fighter. Powered by a 610hp Hispano-Suiza 12Xcrs water-cooled inline engine, the Ki-12 had an estimated top speed of 298mph at optimum altitude and could climb to 16,405ft in 6min 30sec. Armament consisted of one 20mm cannon firing through the hollow propeller shaft and two 7.7mm machine guns in the wings.

The Ki-12 represented, in many ways, the present and future of Japanese fighter design. For the JAAF, however, the new Ki-12, with its streamlined inline engine, failed the one crucial test – maneuverability. At the same time Nakajima was working on the Ki-27, a fighter well suited to the JAAF's requirements. Duly chosen as its next fighter, the superbly maneuverable Type 97 Ki-27 was ordered into production in late 1937. An all-metal monoplane, but with a fixed, spatted undercarriage, the Ki-27 was fitted with just two 7.7mm machines guns. Its meager armament was no better than that of the Sopwith Camel of World War I. However, the Ki-27's performance and success in Japan's war with China and the USSR in the late 1930s only solidified the JAAF's belief in the lightweight maneuverable fighter.

A stripped airframe reveals the skeletal structure of the Ki-44 as maintenance apprentices listen attentively to their instructor at the Tokorozawa Army Maintenance Technical School. The latter held instructional airframes of most aircraft types in JAAF service. The large hatch in the fuselage was primarily to provide access to the radio equipment. Good serviceability rates in any fighter unit were vital for success. As the war progressed the shortage of good repair and maintenance personnel, along with dedicated facilities and spare parts, greatly reduced the effectiveness of most JAAF fighter units. (Picarella Collection)

Combat, however, tended to reveal one weakness. From May 11 to September 15, 1939, the JAAF battled the Soviet Red Air Force during the Nomonhan Incident along the Mongolian–Manchurian border. Ki-27s claimed more than 1,000 communist aircraft destroyed for the loss of 63 pilots killed. Soviet pilots soon learned, like American, Dutch, Australian, and British aviators during World War II, to avoid slow-turning dogfights. Using "dive-and-zoom" tactics, Soviet pilots, flying the latest Polikarpov I-16 armed with two ShVAK 20mm cannon, managed to best the more nimble Ki-27s on a number of occasions. That experience led the JAAF to question its faith in lightweight, maneuverable fighters. Many Japanese pilots realized that fighter combat was changing from the horizontal into the vertical plain. The demand for an aircraft with more speed, heavier armament, and the ability to climb and dive was now at hand.

As the Ki-27 entered service Nakajima began work on its replacement, the Ki-43. The new Ki-43 Type 1 Fighter Hayabusa was to have retractable landing gear, a fully enclosed cockpit, and improved armament. It would be the JAAF's last lightweight fighter. With work well underway, the Koku Hombu (Air Headquarters of the

Ki-44-II HEI SHOKI

Japanese Army) began to hedge its bets. Not ready to completely abandon the primacy of maneuverability, it conceived a new heavy fighter to complement the Ki-43. It had to be capable of bringing down new Allied bombers like the Consolidated B-24 Liberator, North American B-25, and Martin B-26 Marauder, all of which were then in development.

When the Ki-43 entered service trials, the Koku Hombu asked Nakajima to commence work on the new heavy fighter, which would be designated the Ki-44 Type 2 single-seat fighter. It was required to have a maximum speed of 373mph at 13,120ft and be able to attain an altitude of 16,500ft less than five minutes after takeoff. Armament was increased to two 12.7mm Ho-103 and two 7.7mm Type 89 machine guns.

Work on the Ki-44 commenced in 1938 under the leadership of Yasushi Koyama. To meet the JAAF's challenging performance requirements, Nakajima chose its own Ha-41 two-row, 14-cylinder radial rated at 1,250hp. Like most Japanese fighters, the Ki-44 was equipped with a two-speed single stage supercharger. To accommodate the large Ha-41 engine the design team created a stubby-winged fighter with a small airframe. "Butterfly flaps" were added to enhance maneuverability, these being designed to increase wing area without increasing drag. Regular flaps increase wing area but also create drag that slows the aircraft down when they are deployed. Because of the way that "butterfly" flaps (and Fowler flaps, which were similar in concept although they also dropped downwards when deployed) extended backwards from the wing, they could be opened at higher speeds than standard flaps.

Flight tests of the first prototype (Nakajima c/n 4401) began in August 1940. Unfortunately, the prototype was overweight. Estimated to have a fully loaded weight of about 4,850lb, the first prototype weighed in at 5,622lb. Flight performance was disappointing as well. Top speed was lower than hoped for and the landing speed was higher than that of the Ki-43. The aircraft was simply too heavy and produced too much drag. With a maximum speed of just 342mph, it was immediately subjected to a series of design changes. The cowling flaps and supercharger intake were modified (the supercharger intake was modified six times) and the rigidity of the engine mounts was strengthened as well. Unarmed, the newly modified prototype reached a top speed of 389mph at 13,120ft. This, however, was misleading, and the Koku Hombu estimated that production aircraft fully equipped with armor, self-sealing tanks, and full armament would be able to reach 360mph. The design was then frozen, Nakajima being ordered to complete the pre-production aircraft and bring the second and third prototypes up to standard.

Completed in the summer of 1941, the seven pre-production Ki-44s were armed with two 7.7mm Type 89 machine guns on the upper forward fuselage and two 12.7mm Type 1 Ho-103 machine guns in the wings outboard of the main undercarriage.

To speed up operational deployment, all seven pre-production aircraft and the two modified prototypes were issued to the 47th Dokuritsu Hikō Chutai (47th Independent Air Company). Unofficially known as the Kawasemi Butai (Kingfisher Force), the new unit was sent to Saigon prior to the outbreak of war on December 7, 1941.

In terms of performance, the Ki-44 was comparable to the best British, German, and American designs in mid-1941. A little over a year later, the JAAF conducted evaluation

OPPOSITE

This unpainted Ki-44-II Hei was the personal aircraft of WO Makoto Ogawa of the 70th Hikō Sentai, the ace flying it from Kashiwa during the spring of 1945. One of the most successful B-29 killers in the JAAF, he would survive the war with claims for seven Superfortresses and two P-51Ds destroyed. Ogawa's Shoki was marked with an elaborate black eagle for each of his B-29 claims. After seven years of combat Ogawa had attained a high level of proficiency that allowed him to develop two methods of attack when engaging Superfortresses. During night missions, he would close on them head on and below, while during day interceptions he would only attack once the bombers had started to drop their ordnance – forced to fly straight and level at this critical point in the mission, they made easy targets for Ogawa.

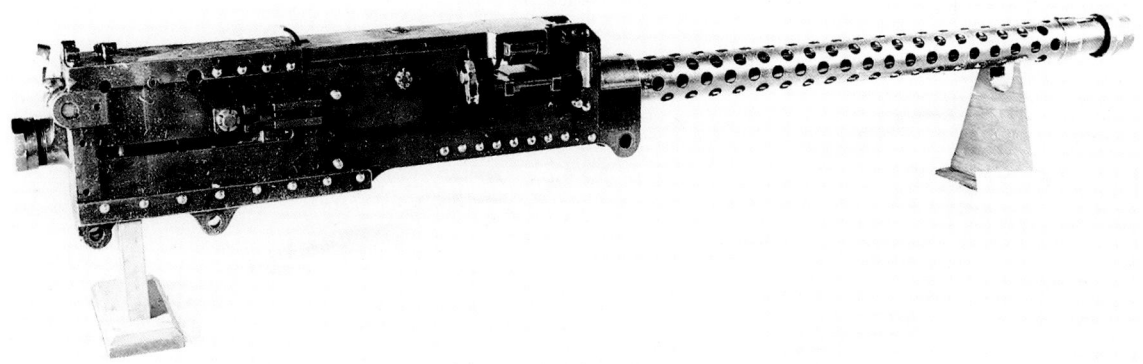

The Ho-103 12.7mm machine gun was recoil-operated, assisted by a muzzle recoil booster, air cooled and belt-fed. Weighing in at approximately 51lb, the Ho-103 fired both high-explosive and armor-piercing rounds. (National Museum of the USAF)

trials at Kakamigahara in September 1942 that pitted a standard production Ki-44-I Otsu against the Kawasaki Ki-61, Nakajima Ki-43-II, Messerschmitt Bf 109E, and a captured Curtiss P-40E. The Ki-61 proved to be the overall winner, but the Shoki was superior to both the Bf 109E and P-40E. Indeed, during high-speed diving trials the Ki-44 reached a speed of 528mph without it suffering any adverse structural effects.

Reports being sent back by the 47th Chutai were promising enough to convince the Koku Hombu to commit the type to series production – 40 were ordered in January 1942, designated Ki-44-I and given the name Shoki. Similar to the pre-production version, the new variant was quickly up-gunned with four 12.7mm Ho-103 machine guns and designated as the Ki-44-I Ko.

While accepted for production, the Ki-44 still lacked the top speed stipulated in the original specification. In an attempt to attain this, one Shoki was modified with a pair of two-bladed contra-rotating propellers, but it met with little success. The need for a more powerful engine was obvious, and the Ki-44-II was duly equipped with a Nakajima Ha-109 rated at 1,520hp. Although the new powerplant was longer than the previous Ha-41, no major modifications were required for its fitment. As a result, the new variant was only 50mm longer overall. Speed increased to 376mph at 17,060ft. In addition to the new engine, other improvements included greater fuel capacity, better landing gear hydraulics, thicker pilot armor, and improved self-sealing tanks. Although mass production began in January 1943, fewer than 250 Ki-44s had been completed by August of that year.

The aircraft's excellent dive and climb characteristics allowed the JAAF to develop fast "hit and run" tactics. The Shoki was also a superb gun platform. Trading height for speed and speed for altitude proved a radical departure from the "traditional" JAAF "dogfighting" tactics. Pilots who transitioned from the more nimble Ki-27 and Ki-43, and were able to embrace the Shoki's best qualities, proved to be deadly opponents.

Like their Allied contemporaries, Nakajima's aircraft designers were constantly looking for ways to improve the Shoki. As production of the Ki-44-II rose to 50–60 aircraft per month, work on the Ki-44-III Ko began in early 1943. Powered by the 2,000hp Nakajima Ha-145 18-cyclinder engine, the new version was to be armed with four 20mm Ho-5 cannon. Six pre-production airframes were produced and evaluation of the Ki-44-III was completed by late 1943. However, the aircraft's inferiority to the new Nakajima Ki-84 Hayate resulted in development of the Ki-44-III being terminated by the Koku Hombu. The Ki-44-II, however, would remain in production until January 1945. The next variant to reach the frontline was the Ki-44-II Otsu. Armed with two 12.7mm Ho-103 machine guns in the fuselage and a pair of wing-mounted 40mm Ho-301 cannon, it was one of the most heavily armed single-seat JAAF fighters of the war. The Ho-301 cannon's low velocity and short range required a point-blank approach – a near suicidal tactic against the B-29. By March 1944 Nakajima had produced 394 examples.

As a bomber interceptor, the Ki-44 was at a distinct disadvantage due to its light armament. Indeed, early Luftwaffe experience had revealed that it took at least 20 rounds of 20mm cannon fire to bring down a B-17 or B-24. Instead of just four 12.7mm machine guns, the Ki-44's armament should have included at least two 20mm cannon from the outset. This shortcoming was again ignored with the last production variant of the Shoki, the Ki-44-II Hei. In fact, Nakajima took a step backwards by fitting it with just four 12.7mm Ho-103 machine guns. On a more positive note, these late-production machines had the new 100-Shiki (Type 100) reflector gunsight fitted as standard. Just 427 examples of the Ki-44-II Hei were built between March 1944 and January 1945. The proposed Ki-44-III Otsu version would have addressed the armament issues, with the fighter boasting four 20mm cannon or two 20mm cannon and two Ho-203 37mm weapons. Just one prototype was constructed in January 1945, however, it being the last Shoki ever built.

The Allies got their first good look at two crashed Ki-44s in China in 1943. US Intelligence noted that the "Tojo" (the aircraft's Allied reporting name) "was not so maneuverable as the 'Zeke' or 'Oscar,' but much faster in a dive, climb and level flight." The Ki-44 pilot's manual "listed restrictions on spins, snap-rolls, quick turns, sudden zooms at high speed and accelerations greater than 5gs. Combat reports indicated that these restrictions are not respected by Jap[anese] pilots!"

Unfortunately for the JAAF, the Ki-44 was never considered superior to the Ki-43. Whereas some 5,819 examples of the latter machine were built, just 1,225 Shokis were completed by Nakajima.

Three pre-production and three prototype Ki-44s are seen here lined up alongside a single Kawasaki Ki-60 fighter at Tama airfield during flight testing. Tama, as home to the Air Test Department, was the center of all JAAF flight testing during the war. In June 1944, when air raids started to pose a real threat to Japan, many fighter aircraft assigned to the Air Test Department's Evaluation and Maintenance divisions were armed and pressed into service, including a small number of Ki-44s. (National Museum of the USAF)

TECHNICAL SPECIFICATIONS

B-29 SUPERFORTRESS

When first designed, the B-29 was the world's most complex production aircraft. In terms of performance, it was leaps and bounds ahead of both the vaunted B-17 and versatile B-24. Nevertheless, as advanced as the Superfortress was, its construction was of conventional standards, being all-metal throughout and with fabric-covered control surfaces. All the variants that flew in World War II were powered by the Wright R-3350 engine driving a Hamilton Standard full-feathering constant-speed propeller – some specialist models were fitted with four-bladed Curtiss-Wright electric constant-speed, feathering and reversing propellers.

During production the B-29 experienced a phenomenal number of changes to its original specification. To reduce the impact of these modifications on the manufacturing process, the USAAF used a production block system for all aircraft types. All airframes in a set production block (normally 50 or 100) would be constructed to the agreed specification at the start of the block. This maintained a steady output of finished aircraft. Each production block had a code for the manufacturing site added at the end – e.g. B-29-15-BW means the 50 B-29s built by Boeing at its Wichita plant belonged to production block 15. Each aircraft plant was also given its own code – BO for Boeing Seattle, BW for Boeing Wichita, BN for Boeing Renton, MO for Martin Omaha, and BA for Bell Atlanta.

XB-29

Three XB-29s were built at the Boeing Seattle, Washington, plant in 1942. The first, 41-002, made its maiden flight on September 21, 1942. Each was equipped with four R-3350-12s engines and 17ft-diameter three-bladed propellers, with no armament fitted. Plagued by chronic engine overheating problems, the first prototype required 16 powerplant changes, 19 exhaust system modifications, and 22 carburetors swapped out. XB-29 41-002 remained as a test airframe throughout the war.

The second prototype (41-003) flew for the first time on December 30, 1942 and crashed on February 18, 1943, killing all onboard. The third prototype (41-18335) did not take to the air until June 1943, after numerous changes were made to it in an attempt to solve some of the problems that had afflicted the first two prototypes. These included extensive powerplant and equipment revisions. It too would crash, however. Despite the mechanical maladies that beset the XB-29s, the aircraft's handling qualities had proven to be so good that no significant aerodynamic changes were required.

YB-29

The YB-29s were service test aircraft, with 14 examples being built at Wichita, Kansas – the first, YB-29 (41-36954), left the production line on April 15, 1943. Powered by four R-3350-21 engines driving three-bladed propellers (which were soon replaced by "four-bladers" in the field), it took to the air for the first time on June 26, 1943. Several YB-29s were used extensively to test various alternative remote-sighted turret systems. Armament was finally standardized at ten 0.50-cal machine guns and one 20mm cannon in four remote turrets and the manned tail turret.

Ongoing trouble with the R-3350 led the first YB-29 to be used as a test bed for the liquid-cooled Allison V-3420-17. Equipped with four such engines, it was later re-designated the XB-39. The V-3420-17 was essentially a pair of Allison V-1710s coupled to a single propeller shaft and developing an impressive 2,100hp at 25,000ft. Speed increased to 405mph at 25,000ft, but by the time the engines were tested the B-29 was already in combat. Changing engines in the middle of production made no sense, resulting in the XB-39 being a one off.

Two YB-29s in flight, with the aircraft nearest to the camera being the seventh production example, 41-36960. Both aircraft are equipped with the GE gun turret system, and they also have silver strips on the leading edges of the wings, fin, and tail where the de-icer boots should be. (National Museum of the USAF)

The three-gun arrangement (one 20mm cannon and two 0.50-cal machine guns) in the tail of the B-29 provided a staggering amount of firepower. Unfortunately, the bullet trajectories between the cannon and machine guns did not match, making it difficult to hit an enemy fighter with projectiles from all three weapons at the same time. (Author's Collection)

The first unit to receive the B-29 was the 58th BW, activated at Marietta, Georgia, on June 1, 1943. The following month it received seven YB-29s so that crew training could commence.

B-29

The B-29 was the major production version of the Superfortress and the first to see combat. Of the 2,848 examples built, 1,644 were produced by Boeing, 536 by Martin, and 668 by Bell. Visually, the B-29 was almost identical to the late-version YB-29. The new B-29 was equipped with four R-3350-23, -23A or, later, -41 engines, with a war emergency rating of 2,300hp, driving four 16ft 7in diameter fully feathering four-bladed propellers. The crew consisted of the pilot (later aircraft commander), co-pilot, flight engineer, bombardier, navigator, radar operator, radio operator, and four CFC gunners. The first seven were located in the forward pressurized cabin. The remaining four gunners were located just aft of the trailing edge of the wing, with the tail gunner in a separate pressurized compartment.

The wingspan of the B-29 was 141ft 3in. Designated the Boeing 117 aerofoil, it had a very high aspect ratio of 11.5. Long and narrow, the high aspect ratio wing enabled the B-29 to fly fast at high altitude and provide good flight characteristics

When not operating the Norden bombsight, the bombardier was responsible for the forward defense of the aircraft. With the least amount of gunnery training, the bombardier had to deal with terrifying and deadly head-on attacks. The frontal area of the Ki-44 was very small, and hitting one when coming head on, with a combined closing speed of more than 600mph, proved extremely difficult. (National Museum of the USAF)

B-29 GE TURRET

The B-29's remote GE turrets were compact and streamlined, but had one distinct disadvantage according to an anonymous gunner. "Because the guns are mounted where you can't easily get at them in flight, a malfunction is hard to repair – often impossible – once you leave the ground. If one of your '.50-cals' stops working, it may be out for the duration of the mission." Each Browning M2 0.50-cal machine gun was supplied with 500 rounds of ammunition.

during the slower speeds required for takeoff and landing. Combat range with a 5,000lb bomb load was 3,250 miles with a standard fuel load of 6,940 gallons.

Early encounters with Japanese fighters revealed the need for more protection against head-on attacks, so the front dorsal turret was up-gunned to four 0.50-cal machine guns. This modification appeared on B-29s from block 40 onwards at the Boeing Wichita facility, from block 10 at the Bell Atlanta plant, and on all Martin-built B-29s from the very beginning.

Early models of the B-29 carried the Philco AN/APN-4 LORAN (LOng RANge) constant-beam navigation aid. This was replaced by the more accurate RCA AN/APN-9 system later in the war. The B-29 was also equipped with the AN/APQ-13 radar bombing/navigation set. Housed inside a 30in hemispherical radome, it was located between the two bomb bays. The AN/APQ-13 would in turn be replaced by the AN/APQ-7 Eagle radar later in the war.

B-29A

The B-29A was identical to the previous model in every respect except for the wing construction and the method employed to attach it to the fuselage. The B-29 used a two-piece wing center section that was bolted together at the center line and installed as a single unit. Passing through the fuselage, it supported the engine nacelles. On the

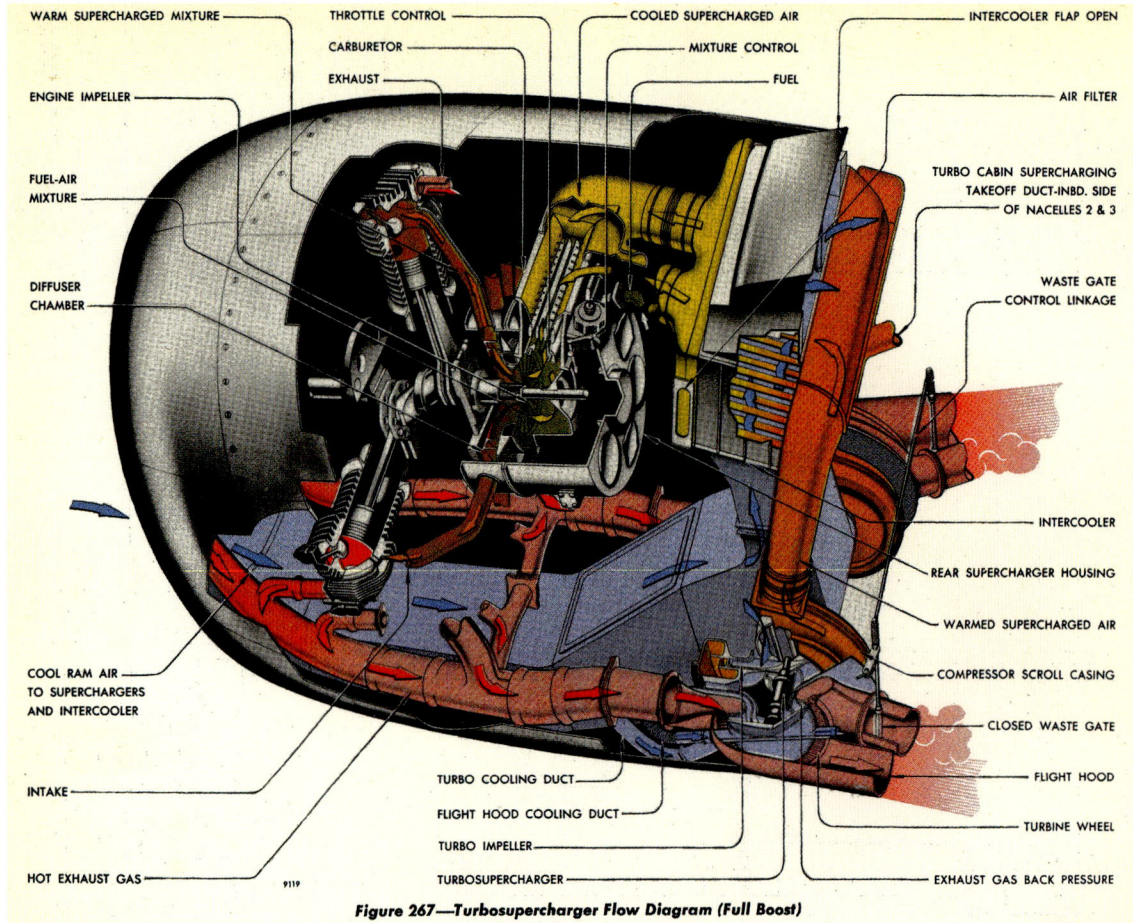

Figure 267—Turbosupercharger Flow Diagram (Full Boost)

All American heavy bombers during World War II were equipped with turbo-superchargers. Taken from the B-29 pilot's flight manual, this cutaway drawing graphically illustrates the flow of air and gases in the aircraft's turbo-supercharger. Each Wright R-3350 was equipped with two turbos, giving the B-29 exceptional high-altitude performance. (Author's Collection)

B-29A a short stub center section projected only a modest distance beyond the fuselage, and the wings were bolted on at station 47.75. This modified construction method reduced the aircraft's fuel load by some 200 gallons, which was not popular with Maj Gen LeMay. Numerous aviation publications state that because of the different manufacturing method, the B-29A's wing was a foot longer than the B-29's. This is completely false. Official USAAF documentation quotes an identical single wingspan – 141ft 3in – for both the B-29 and the B-29A.

Powered by four R-3350-57 engines, the B-29A was armed with 12 0.50-cal machine guns. The front dorsal turret was up-gunned to four such weapons, while the 20mm cannon was removed from the tail turret altogether.

All 1,119 B-29As built were constructed at Boeing's Renton plant.

B-29B

Similar to the B-29, the B-29B was easily recognized by its lack of turrets. All defensive armament was removed except for the two tail guns, with smooth fairings covering all vacant turret and sighting stations. The "lightened" version had a top speed of 364mph at 25,000ft. The tail turret was equipped with AN/APG-15B gun laying radar. The latter, however, proved troublesome and ineffective and was soon removed from most aircraft. A total of 311 B-29Bs were built, with most being issued to XXI Bomber Command's 315th BW at Guam.

B-29C
The B-29C was similar to the B-29 but with improved R-3350 engines fitted. No fewer than 5,000 were originally ordered, but the USAAF cancelled these aircraft immediately after VJ-Day.

F-13
The F-13 was the photo-reconnaissance version of the B-29A/B. Retaining all bombing and defensive armament, the aircraft was equipped with a suite of six cameras in the rear pressurized compartment. The cameras carried included a vertically mounted Fairchild K-18 for general photographic work, two K-22s on a split vertical mount, and three K-17Bs in a trimetrogon mount for photo-mapping.

The first F-13A to arrive in the Marianas was 42-93852 *TOKYO ROSE* of the 3rd Photographic Reconnaissance Squadron (PRS) on October 13, 1944. On November 1, 1944, it became the first Allied aircraft to fly over Tokyo since the "Doolittle Raid" in April 1942.

B-29 SUPERFORTRESS FIELDS-OF-FIRE

Standard armament for the B-29 and B-29A was 12 M-2 0.50-cal machine guns housed in four remote turrets and the tail position (the front dorsal turret was armed with four guns and the rest carried two each). The tail turret originally boasted two 0.50-cals and a single M2 20mm cannon, but by early 1945 the latter weapon was no longer in use. Each 0.50-cal gun was provided with 500 rounds of ammunition. The B-29's defensive field-of-fire was exceptional, covering every aspect of the aircraft. One of the most unique features of the bomber's CFC system was its ability to allow a single gunner to control two turrets at the same time, doubling the firepower. Taught to fire short bursts, a single gunner controlling the two top turrets (six guns in total) could unleash approximately 150 projectiles in one two-second burst.

SB-29

The SB-29 "Super Dumbo" was the air-sea rescue (ASR) version of the Superfortress. In the last few months of the war 15 B-29s and one B-29A were modified to carry a droppable A-3 Edo lifeboat beneath the fuselage. All defensive armament was retained except for the lower forward turret, which was replaced by an AN/APQ-13 radome.

SILVERPLATE B-29

Built by the Glenn L. Martin factory, 46 *Silverplate* B-29s were produced before the end of the war. Twenty-nine were assigned to the 509th CG, with 15 based in the Marianas. All were stripped of turrets and armor, but retained the twin 0.50-cal machine guns in the tail. Each was equipped with four fuel-injected R-3350-41 engines and Curtiss-Electric reversible pitch propellers – a new technology. The bomb-bays of each B-29 were reconfigured so that a 10,000lb bomb – more specifically an atomic bomb – could be suspended from a single point. British F-type bomb release and G-type attachments, along with dual electrical and mechanical bomb release mechanisms, were installed. Pneumatic actuators were also fitted for rapid opening and closing of the bomb-bay doors. In addition to the bombardier, a new crew position was created called the "weaponeer station." His job was to monitor the release and detonation of the atomic weapons.

Ki-44 SHOKI

The Ki-44 has to be considered as the first true interceptor in the JAAF. The initial concept for the fighter was put forward in 1938, although design and construction work by engineer Yasushi Koyama's team (which included Shigenobu Mori, Masataro Uchida, and Hideo Itokawa) did not commence until June 1939. The Ki-44 was a single-seat, all-metal, low-wing monoplane fighter. Its wing was a two-spar structure with a stressed-skin covering and fabric-covered control services. The wing area was just 161.458 sq ft, with a wingspan of 31ft (the Bf 109F had a wingspan of 32ft 6.5in and a wing area of 172.76 sq ft). Trailing edge "butterfly" flaps produced extra combat maneuverability and additional lift for takeoff and landing, these being actuated by a switch on the pilot's control column.

The oval-shaped, stress-skinned covered fuselage was designed to be as small as possible in cross-section, while the tailplane was an all-metal structure that was again stress-skinned, minus the fabric-covered control services. To improve the Ki-44's handling, the fin and rudder were mounted well back from the horizontal tail surfaces. Beneath a two-piece canopy, the pilot was equipped with a Type 89 optical telescopic gunsight. The undercarriage was fully retractable, with the main wheels folding inward and lying flat under the fuselage center section and the tailwheel retracting backwards.

All Shokis were built by the Nakajima Hikoki KK at its Ota plant, with the final production model coming off the line in December 1944, the Ki-44 being the 44th airframe (or kitai) number designed for the JAAF. The listing commenced in 1932, and subsequent engine or airframe modifications were designated by a Roman numeral suffix – e.g. Ki-44-I and Ki-44-II. Armament changes would add a further suffix, with

Ko, Otsu, and Hei being used with the Ki-44. These suffixes are often represented in lower case letters a, b, c, etc.

To make aircraft recognition easier for Allied servicemen and to avoid using the longer and potentially confusing formal Japanese designations, the Allies adopted boys' names (e.g. "Tony") for fighters and girls' names (e.g. "Betty") for bombers. Inexplicably ignoring this well-established reporting system, the Allies christened the Ki-44 "Tojo" after the Japanese wartime premier, Hideki Tojo.

Ki-44 PROTOTYPE

Three Ki-44 prototypes (production numbers 4401 to 4403) were built, and the first example was flown in August 1940. Powered by a Nakajima Ha-41 twin-row, 14-cylinder radial engine developing 1,250hp, the aircraft's initial performance figures were disappointing. Maximum speed was just 342mph at 13,120ft, some 31mph slower than specified, and the rate of climb to 16,400ft was 54 seconds longer than the desired five minutes. Modifications quickly followed that saw the prototype fitted with more rigid engine mounts, reshaped cowling flaps, and a redesigned supercharger air intake. With the armament removed and a loaded weight of just 5,180lb, the Ki-44 managed to achieve 354mph at 13,120ft. Further modifications followed, with the supercharger air intake redesigned six times. Additional changes to the cowling flaps and the installation of a firewall eliminated the need for cooling vents around the upper fuselage. These changes increased the top speed to 389mph, but again this was without the aircraft being fully armed. Satisfied, the Koku Hombu froze the design and ordered the first batch of pre-production aircraft.

Ki-44 PRE-PRODUCTION

The seven pre-production Ki-44s (production numbers 4404 to 4410) differed little from the three modified prototypes. The new aircraft featured a simplified canopy, a relocated radio aerial (moved from the cockpit canopy to the starboard side of the fuselage), and plumbing and hard points for two 28.6-gallon drop tanks under the center wing section. Armament consisted of two Type 89 7.7mm machine guns, each with 500 rounds, firing through the propeller arc and two Ho-103 12.7mm machine guns in the wings. The latter had a muzzle velocity of 2,657ft/sec and a rate of fire of 900 rounds per minute. The Ho-103s had a 250-round magazine in each wing.

Arguably the best Japanese fighter machine gun of the war, the Ho-103 was a simplified version of the US Model 1921 Browning 0.50-cal machine gun. The weapon fired the less powerful Italian 12.7mm 81sR cartridge, which allowed the gun to be lighter than the Browning, boast a higher rate of fire and improved muzzle velocity. Nevertheless, the Ki-44, even when fitted with a pair of Ho-103s, had an inferior weight of fire compared with its contemporaries at the time. As for the Type 89 7.7mm machine guns, they were all but useless against the well-constructed and heavily armored American fighters and heavy bombers. On the plus side, the Ki-44 was arguably the best gun platform fielded by either the JAAF or the IJNAF in World War II.

Completed in the summer of 1941, the seven pre-production aircraft, along with two fully modified prototypes, were issued to the 47th Hikō Chutai for combat evaluation. Testing also began at Tama airfield (now the USAF's Yokota air base), home of the JAAF's Air Test Department, near the city of Fussa in western Tokyo. For

Ki-44-II KO COWLING/WING GUNS

The Ki-44-II Ko's armament of two cowling-mounted Type 89 7.7mm machine guns (each with magazines containing 500 rounds per weapon) and two wing-mounted Ho-103 12.7mm machine guns (250 rounds per weapon) was extremely light when compared with that of Allied fighters. Rate of fire for the 12.7mm weapon was 800rpm, while the synchronized 7.7mm gun was just 400rpm. As anti-bomber armament, these guns were all but useless. Even when equipped with four 12.7mm guns, the Ki-44 was still at a disadvantage when attempting to shoot down the B-29.

pilots used to the benign handling qualities of the Ki-43, the Ki-44 proved to be far more of a handful. Some considered its high landing speed, poor forward visibility, and marginal directional stability at low speeds to be a negative, but for those who learned to exploit its rapid rate of roll and outstanding dive characteristics, the Ki-44 was a deadly fighter. Initially, the Shoki was considered to be a "hot" aircraft that could only be flown by experienced pilots with more than 1,000 hours of flying time to their log books. However, once the fighter was in frontline service, it was found that aviators of relative inexperience could cope with the Ki-44 satisfactorily.

Ki-44-I

In January 1942, with production of the Ki-44-I now underway, the aircraft was christened Shoki in honor of a semi-mythical Taoist temple deity who could destroy or frighten away demons and devils. An initial series of 40 Ki-44-Is (production numbers 111 to 150) had been ordered, these aircraft being nearly identical to the pre-production

This Ki-44-II Hei of the 246th Hikō Sentai was photographed at Taisho airfield in early 1945. After a disastrous campaign in the Philippines, where the unit lost 40 aircraft between November 8 and December 14, 1944, the 246th returned home in January 1945 and subsequently flew air defense sorties over Nagoya, Kobe, Osaka, and Tokyo through to war's end. The 246th specialized in night interception and air-to-air bombing. This aircraft displays the white fuselage and wing bands that adorned fighters assigned to the Home Defense role. (National Museum of the USAF)

airframes. Although the same armament and Type 89 telescopic gunsight were initially retained, the JAAF soon ordered that the 7.7mm machine guns be changed to four 12.7mm Ho-103s. This resulted in the fighter being re-designated the Ki-44-I Ko, which was followed into production by the Ki-44-I Otsu. With the latter aircraft, the oil cooler, which had previously been located within the engine cowling, was moved to the outside and beneath it. The last production batch, designated the Ki-44-I Hei, featured a slightly modified main undercarriage that saw the hinged gear fairings attached to the wing's undersurface rather than to the legs themselves.

Ki-44-II

The Ki-44-II featured the more powerful Nakajima Ha-109 engine that developed 1,520hp on takeoff and was equipped with a single-speed two-stage supercharger. Nevertheless, the high-altitude performance of the Shoki remained poor. At no time does it seem the Japanese considered using methanol-water or nitrous oxide injection systems to give the Ki-44 extra power at altitude. Five prototypes and three pre-production aircraft were ordered.

The first production version, known as the Ki-44-II Ko, was armed with two Type 89 7.7mm machine guns in the upper forward fuselage and two Ho-103 12.7mm guns in the wings. Heavier than the Ki-44-I, the Ki-44-II was also faster, with a top speed of 376mph at 17,060ft and it could climb to 16,400ft in 4min 17sec. These figures made it the best performing Japanese single-seat fighter at that time. A total of 355 Ki-44-II Kos were built between February 1942 and August 1943 (production numbers 1001 to 1355).

The Ho-301 40mm cannon was a heavy weapon, weighing in at 108lb. It fired caseless ammunition, which had a small amount of internal propellant that made each shell more of a small rocket than a conventional round. Primarily an anti-bomber weapon, the Ho-301's low velocity made it useless in the fighter-versus-fighter role. Most Ki-44-II Otsus had their Ho-301s replaced by faster-firing Ho-103 12.7mm machine guns. (NARA)

A Ho-301 40mm round showing the perforated holes in the base of the projectile that allowed the charge to propel it, thus eliminating the need for loose cartridge cases to be ejected from the cannon. Primarily an anti-bomber weapon, the low muzzle velocity of the Ho-301 required the Ki-44 to approach close to its target – a near-suicidal tactic in daylight. The weapon was duly found to be most effective in nocturnal interceptions. (Picarella Collection)

The next variant was the Ki-44-II Otsu armed with two Ho-103 12.7mm machine guns in the upper fuselage and two wing-mounted Ho-301 40mm cannons, with just ten rounds per gun. Weighing 108lb, the Ho-103 was unique in that it used caseless ammunition – each round was in effect a small rocket. Muzzle velocity was 805ft per second, with a limited range of just 490ft. These upgraded machines were referred to as Tokubet su Sobiki (specially equipped) aircraft. The Ho-103 was a potent anti-bomber weapon, although its low rate of fire and low muzzle velocity meant that it could only be fired at very close range. Many Otsu variants flew without the cannon armament, a large number of them being retrofitted with Ho-103 12.7mm machine guns instead. By March 1944 394 Otsus had been delivered (production numbers 1356 to 1749).

The final variant of the Shoki to attain series production was the Ki-44-II Hei. Armament took a step back, with just four Ho-103 12.7mm machines guns (two in the forward cowling firing synchronized through the propeller and one in each wing). A small number of late production machines received the new 100-Shiki (Type 100) reflector gun sight, replacing the older 89-Shiki (Type 89) telescopic gunsight. Performance was slightly improved on a small number of late production aircraft, with the introduction of individual exhaust stacks (one per cylinder). In April 1944 Ki-44 production peaked with 85 aircraft rolling off the production line, with only 427 examples being built between March 1944 and January 1945 (production numbers 1750–2176).

When the Ki-44 first encountered the B-29, the JAAF quickly realized that the fighter was inferior to the twin-engined Mitsubishi Ki-46 and the single-seat Kawasaki Ki-61 in respect to its high-altitude performance. On the plus side, it was superior to the Ki-43 and twin-engined Kawasaki Ki-45 at the altitudes favored by the Superfortress.

The pristine cockpit of a captured Ki-44-II Hei at Clark Field, in the Philippines. This aircraft, equipped with an Army Type 100 reflector gunsight, was manufactured in October 1944. The butts of the cowling-mounted machine guns can be seen protruding into the cockpit on either side of the instrument panel. Unlike most fighters of the period, which had the gun-firing button fitted to the top of the control column, the Ki-44 had the trigger located immediately ahead of the throttle. (National Museum of the USAF)

Ki-44-III

The Ki-44-III was the last development of the Shoki, Nakajima proposing to fit it with four Ho-5 20mm cannon, or two 20mm weapons and two Ho-203 37mm cannon in an attempt to finally address the aircraft's need for heavier anti-bomber armament. Engine power was to be provided by an Ha-145 twin-row 18-cylinder radial generating 2,000hp. To improve takeoff and landing characteristics, the wing area was increased to 204.515 sq ft and the tail surfaces were enlarged. Just a single prototype was built in January 1945.

THE STRATEGIC SITUATION

"There is one thing that is certain – air power has given to the world a means whereby the heart of a nation can be attacked at once without first having to wage an exhaustive war at the nation's frontiers."
Col Harold L. George, Chief of the Air War Plans Division USAAC

In the 1930s and early 1940s both the Japanese and American governments considered air attacks against Japan as a real possibility in any future war. For the Japanese, the credible real aerial threats to the Home Islands came from long-range Soviet bombers (in the 1930s, however, the Red Air Force was not equipped with any sort of effective long-range bomber) that could reach Tokyo from their bases in Vladivostok. The second threat came from the US Navy's Pacific Fleet, with its growing aircraft carrier fleet that would eventually be able to mount strikes against targets on Japanese soil.

For the Japanese, the best defense was offense. The most effective way to neutralize any threat to the Home Islands was territorial expansion. A pre-emptive land operation targeting Soviet bases would neutralize the threat from the northwest, while expansion of the Japanese defensive perimeter in the Pacific would effectively give the Imperial Japanese Navy a defense in depth, forcing the Americans to fight on its terms. Unfortunately for the Japanese people, there was little emphasis placed on improving the country's air defenses at this time due to the military being focused on the coming all-out-war against the Western powers.

For the American military, discussions related to air attacks on Japan had already taken place at least two years before the raid on Pearl Harbor in December 1941.

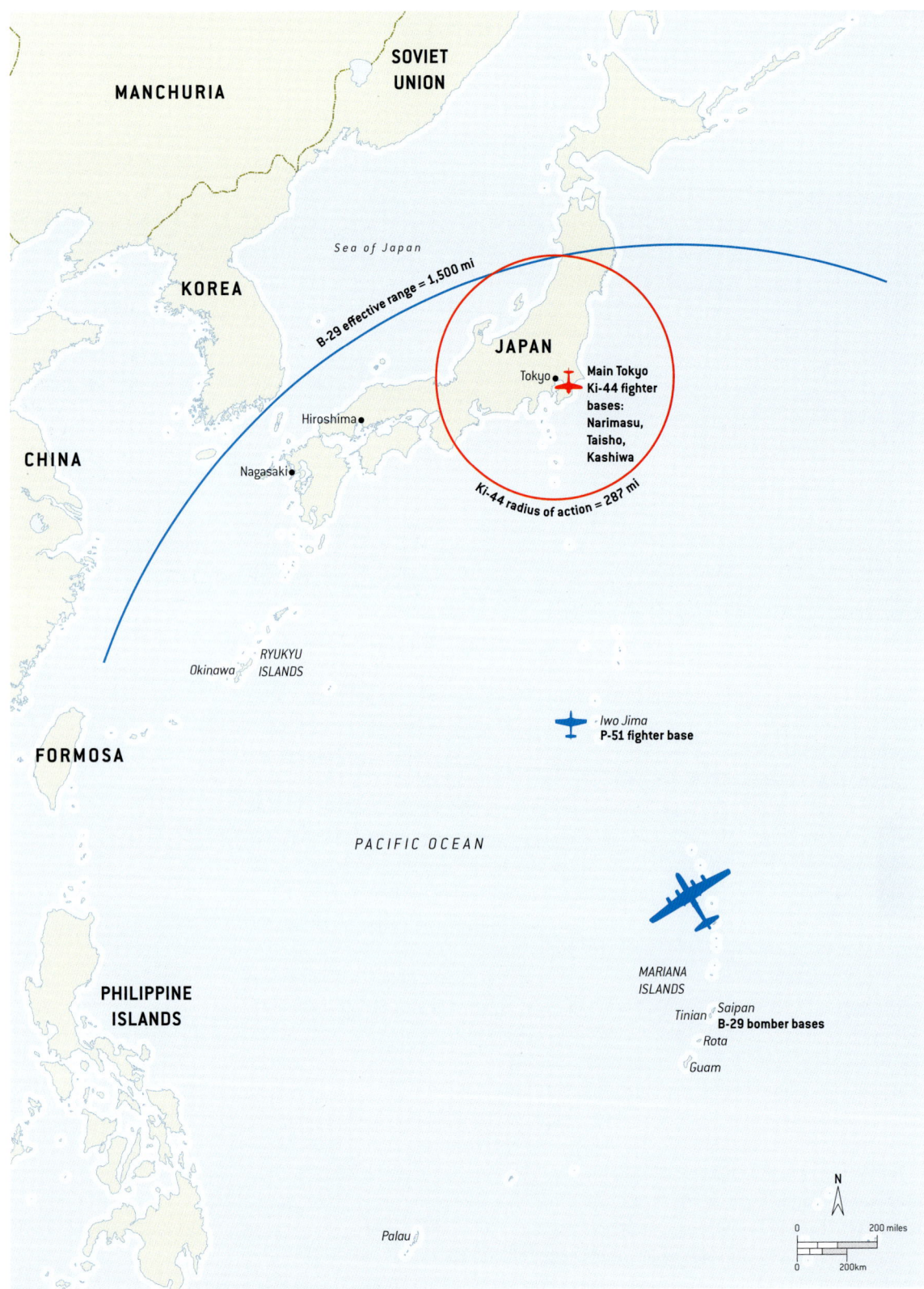

In September of the previous year, Lt Cdr Henri Smith-Hutton, the US naval attaché in Tokyo, had noted that Japan's "firefighting facilities were willfully inadequate. Incendiary bombs sowed widely over an area of Japanese cities would result in the destruction of major portions of the cities." It was a prophetic statement. On March 10–11, 1945, 279 B-29s fire-bombed Tokyo, destroying 16 square miles.

In the winter of 1940–41 the Roosevelt administration, eager to help the Chinese in their war against Japanese expansion, approved the formation of a clandestine fighter group. Staffed by discharged US military personnel, the 1st American Volunteer Group (AVG) would become operational on December 20, 1941. Equipped with Curtiss Tomahawk IIB (P-40B) fighters, the AVG presented the Japanese with their first effective aerial opposition following the attack on Pearl Harbor just 13 days earlier. Although the exploits of the American pilots in their "shark-mouthed" fighters have received considerable coverage over the decades, little mention has been made of the 2nd AVG unit that was due to be formed. It was to be equipped with 33 twin-engined Lockheed Hudsons and an identical number of Douglas DB-7 (A-20) light bombers that were originally built for Britain but acquired by the USAAC in the fall of 1941 as part of the Lend-Lease program in place between the British and US governments.

The Central Aircraft Manufacturing Company, which fronted the Chinese and US governments, recruited 440 air- and groundcrew that would be tasked with flying the first bombing missions against the Japanese Home Islands. However, with America at war with Japan following the Pearl Harbor attack, preparations for the covert bombing of the Home Islands were quickly dropped. American pre-war plans had also envisioned the bombing of Japan from bases on Wake Island, Guam, the Philippines, and along the China coast. Japan's rapid victories in early 1942 all but extinguished those ideas. A new way would have to be found.

The first bombing attack on Japanese soil occurred on April 18, 1942. For the Japanese high command it came as a complete and utter shock. On that day, 16 USAAF B-25B Mitchell medium bombers, led by Lt Col James H. Doolittle, took off from the aircraft carrier USS *Hornet* (CV-8) and headed for Tokyo, Yokohama, Nagoya, and Kobe. It was a bold, daring, successful attack. From a military perspective it inflicted only modest damage, but that was not the point of the mission. Often described as little more than a morale-boosting exercise, the "Doolittle Raid" clearly signaled that much more was to come.

Its psychological effect on the Japanese high command was profound. The very fact that medium bombers appeared in broad daylight over the Home Islands was a sober and humiliating warning. Target selection was also telling. While little damage was expected, USAAF planners largely selected strategic targets for their bombs, which included petroleum facilities, aircraft factories, steel mills, and the Tokyo Gas and Electric Company. More than 26 months would pass before the strategic bombing of Japan began in earnest, however.

Early USAAF war plans had 2,040 B-29s based in Northern Ireland and fully prepared to bomb Germany into submission. However, by 1943, USAAF planners had agreed that the B-29 force would only be used against Japan. This decision would directly shape the strategy of conquest in the central Pacific. While the Superfortress had great range, there were no Allied bases even close to Japan from which it could

OPPOSITE

The Pacific theater of war was the largest of World War II, and as such, it presented B-29 crews with unprecedented challenges. Flying extreme long-range missions from bases in the Mariana Island archipelago required unerring navigation and the routine reliability of a commercial airline. Halfway between the Marianas and Japan, the tiny island of Iwo Jima proved invaluable for returning B-29 crews. During the campaign hundreds of Superfortresses, damaged or short on fuel, made emergency landings on the airstrip here. Without Iwo Jima, B-29 losses would have been considerably higher. By war's end, the USAAF's Superfortress service and repair unit based on Iwo Jima was staffed by almost 2,000 airmen.

B-29 42-24464 *Flying Stud II* was photographed at Dudhkundi airfield, in India, in early 1945. This aircraft was assigned to the 676th BS/444th BG, which was the first group to fly B-29s from forward staging bases – specifically Kwanghan – in China. The bomber boasts an already impressive mission tally, with the camel silhouettes denoting supply missions over "the Hump" and black hearts beneath the bomb symbols reflecting flak damage inflicted on the aircraft. CFC gunners have also been credited with seven victories. *Flying Stud II* moved with the 444th to West Field on Tinian, in the Mariana Islands, during the spring of 1945 after the USAAF lost its forward staging bases in China during Japan's *Ichi-Go* offensive. Having survived in the frontline for almost a year, 42-24464 returned to the USA on June 15, 1945 after being declared War Weary. It was reclaimed at Tinker air force base, Oklahoma, in May 1949. (Author's Collection)

operate. The US Joint Chiefs of Staff ordered the main islands in the Marianas chain to be taken and turned into the forward operating bases for the B-29. Unfortunately, many more battles in 1943–44 would have to be fought before the Marianas would be accessible. This forced the USAAF to select the CBI as the theater in which to give the B-29 its combat debut.

In an operation codenamed *Matterhorn*, Superfortresses would fly missions from forward bases around Chengtu, in China. From here, they could just reach the southern tip of Kyushu. In early April 1944 the first B-29s of the 58th BW began their long ferry flights (11,500 miles) to Calcutta, in India. On June 5 the B-29s of XX Bomber Command flew their first mission. Over the following ten months of operations from India and China, XX Bomber Command would launch 49 missions through to April 1945. Only nine targeted Japan, however.

The JAAF knew the "B-san" would be a future threat. Early news reports in 1943 revealed the death of test pilot Eddie Allen and the crash of "a new Boeing bomber." The Japanese high command was also well aware of the USAAF's intention to mount a strategic bombing campaign against the Home Islands. In response the Imperial General Headquarters directed the JAAF intelligence section to focus on the B-29. Using the probable capabilities of the US aviation industry, JAAF engineers "built" a paper super bomber. By the end of 1943 the JAAF had produced a prescient interim report. It knew the B-29 would be pressurized, with an operational ceiling of 32,800ft. Operating bases would most likely include islands in the western Pacific and China, and missions would begin in May or June 1944.

The Japanese got their first glimpse of the B-29 when aircraft landed in India in April 1944. Up to this point JAAF intelligence had done a remarkable job. Unfortunately for the Japanese population, the defensive preparations made by the JAAF and IJNAF to counter the B-29 would prove anemic at best and soon turn desperate.

In February 1944 the JAAF issued a five-page pamphlet titled *Views on the Use of Crash Tactics in Aerial Protection of Vital Defense Areas – No. 2*. "We are now in a situation where we can demand nothing better than crash tactics which insure the destruction of an enemy airplane at one fell swoop, thus striking terror into his heart and rendering his powerfully armed and well equipped airplanes valueless by the sacrifice of one of our fighters."

By then the nation's military resources were stretched to the limit and beyond. Firmly on the defensive, Japan's only hope of saving itself from aerial destruction was to inflict unacceptable losses upon the B-29 force. To do that the JAAF and IJNAF needed fighters and a large number of well-trained pilots. The aerial battles in the Southwest Pacific, Burma, and China from 1942 through to early 1944 had virtually destroyed both air forces. Lack of fuel curtailed training, sending pilots with just 60 to 70 hours of flight experience into combat, with predictable results. Surprisingly, no more than 26 percent of the total Japanese fighter force was ever assigned to the defense of Japan. By March 1945 Japanese home defense squadrons were equipped with just 500 single-seat and twin-engined fighters.

For the Ki-44 units assigned to the defense of Japan, the B-29 was a formidable foe. Early encounters with the bomber over China showed the Ki-44 to be both poorly armed and lacking sufficient high-altitude performance to engage the Superfortresses.

This Ki-44-II Ko is believed to be one of the aircraft flown by 85th Hikō Sentai ace Yukiyoshi Wakamatsu, and it was photographed in China during 1943. This Shoki variant can be distinguished from the earlier Ko version by the prominent oil cooler beneath the cowling. (National Museum of the USAF)

A Ki-44-II Ko sits ready for evaluation at Tama airfield during the summer of 1942, its Army Type 89 telescopic gunsight being clearly visible. The latter had a rubber eyepiece and a protective cap that could be opened from the cockpit before combat. The use of this type of sight reduced the pilot's situational awareness, however, and the Ki-44-II Otsu was the last version of the Shoki to be equipped with the Type 89. Subsequent models had the Army Type 100 reflector gunsight fitted instead. (National Museum of the USAF)

This view of Guam's North Field was taken in the early spring of 1945, with its flight line crammed full of B-29s from the 29th BG's 314th BW. The 29th BG was identified by the enclosed "O" in a black square, the group arriving on Guam between February 15 and 26, 1945. It would go on to fly 66 combat missions. (National Museum of the USAF)

Just four home island defense sentais (23rd, 47th, 70th, and 246th) from the 10th Hikō-Shiden (Air Division) were equipped with the Ki-44. Attrition in the Shoki units fighting in China alone barely kept pace with replacement aircraft, for between January and December 1944 only 565 Ki-44s were produced – an average of just 47 aircraft per month. In sharp contrast, production of the B-29 ran at more than 100 bombers per month during the same period. After the invasion and capture of the Marianas, the Japanese aviation industry began a panic-fueled dispersal effort. This led to dramatically reduced engine and fighter production. Sentai serviceability rates also suffered due to a lack of spare parts, fuel, and trained mechanics, and this in turn saw aircraft availability rates drop to just 45 percent in some units.

In February 1945 US Navy Task Force 38 began air strikes in and around the Tokyo area. Japanese fighter units, including those equipped with Ki-44s, were forced to engage the well-trained, carrier-based, fighter pilots of the US Navy and US Marine Corps. The appearance of F6F Hellcats and F4U Corsairs over Tokyo just added to the stress and strain for the Ki-44 units charged with defending the Home Islands. Pilot fatigue and morale suffered, greatly decreasing the Ki-44's effectiveness as a fighter.

On November 24, 1944, XXI Bomber Command mounted the first B-29 raid on Japan from its bases on Saipan. From that point forward the Japanese saw an ever increasing number of Superfortresses flying both day and night over the Home Islands. Starting on April 7, 1945, Iwo Jima-based long-range P-51Ds and P-47Ns made their first appearance over Japan. USAAF long-range escort fighters and carrier-based US Navy fighters mounting sweeps over the Home Islands quickly crippled what was left of the Japanese air defense forces. By June 1945 all JAAF fighter units had been ordered to conserve their strength for the anticipated invasion of Japan.

Four B-29s from the 9th BG's 99th BS head out for Japan from their base on Tinian in the spring of 1945. The nearest aircraft to the camera is B-29 44-70072 *Limber Richard*, which joined the 99th BS at the very end of April 1945 and duly completed 30 combat missions prior to returning to the USA on June 17, 1946. The 9th BG B-29s were identified by their white-painted fin tips and engine cowlings. (National Museum of the USAF)

THE COMBATANTS

"The protection aerial gunners provide is vital to the success of long-range bombing. On his ability of self-protection, long-range bombing is built. Each bomber, alone, must be able to hold its own against fighters. Everything depends on the ability of one special class of men – the aerial gunners."
Las Vegas Army Airfield Year Book, 1943

USAAF AIR GUNNERY TRAINING

During World War II the air gunner was considered a vital cog in the success of the strategic bombing campaign against both Germany and Japan. American and British pre-war theory envisioned heavily armed bombers flying in tight "combat box" formations fighting off enemy fighter attacks, finding and bombing their targets effectively and returning home. It was good in theory, but the reality would prove far more disappointing.

After World War I air gunner training in the USA had all but disappeared. Its first revival began at Wright Field in 1927, when three flexible gunnery ranges were built. As aircraft became faster, and with the introduction of the revolutionary Martin B-10 all-metal monoplane bomber in November 1934, gunners found it more difficult to track and hit targets with their outdated equipment. With the introduction of the Boeing B-17 from April 1938, the USAAC slowly began to focus on the training of aerial gunners to man the bomber's many guns. By the late 1930s various forms of aerial gunnery were being taught at six different schools scattered across the country. With war approaching, the USAAC began steps to expand and modernize its air force and training programs.

Gunnery practice in San Diego, California. Using a mix of free mount 0.50-cal machine guns and truck-mounted turrets, trainees blast away at towed targets. B-29 gunners were encouraged to fire in short bursts, and to cool their guns at every opportunity by moving the barrels into the slipstream. (National Museum of the USAF)

When war broke out in Europe in September 1939 the USAAC had no training facilities dedicated to aerial gunnery. A year later, with plans having been drawn up to establish two flexible gunnery schools, the USAAC sent a team to Britain to see what the RAF was doing. A report submitted in October by Maj W. L. Kennedy recommended a number of vital requirements as follows – prepare well-trained instructors; provide gunner trainees with extensive firing opportunities at aerial targets; use synthetic training devices; assign fighter aircraft to gunnery schools to conduct simulated fighter attacks with gunners using gun cameras; and award distinctive aerial gunner's wings to trainees upon graduation.

In 1941 the very first flexible gunnery school was established north of Las Vegas, Nevada. The site was ideal for gunnery training, with excellent flying weather and large uninhabited desert expanses that were perfect for ground and aerial gunnery ranges. After the Pearl Harbor attack five more gunnery schools would be established.

Gunnery training began with a four-week course (later extended to six weeks), initial classroom instruction focusing on machine guns, maintenance, cleaning, and how to tear down and reassemble the guns blindfolded. Next, the new trainee would practice using air rifles for marksmanship, shooting shotguns at clay pigeons on the ground and from moving trucks, followed by stationary machine gun firing. The next step was ground turret firing at towed flags. During the first stage of training students did not know what type of bomber or which gunner's position they would be assigned, which in turn meant that they had to be proficient with every type of turret then in use.

With preliminary ground training complete, the gunners duly took to the air. Strapped into the back of an AT-6 Texan, trainees took aim at towed target sleeves from different angles and approaches. The next step was air firing from a B-34 Lexington (reverse Lend-Lease Ventura IIs originally ordered for the RAF but retained by the USAAF following the Pearl Harbor raid) or B-26 Marauder using the Browning M-2 0.50-cal machine gun.

The USAAF air gunnery syllabus would also see the use of ingenious simulators or synthetic trainers. The first was the Hunt Trainer, which allowed the instructor to move a model aircraft relative to the gunner's position via an array of mirrors. It was the gunner's job to judge the distance from his gun to the moving model. The next simulator was the Jam Handy. Using two synchronized film projectors, footage of fighter attacks and breakaways were shown on one projector while the other cast a spotlight in the shape of a ring sight with the correct aiming point. The gunner aimed a 0.50-cal weapon that had been fitted with an optical sight. When the student "fired" the gun, a light dot appeared on the screen showing his aiming point.

The most sophisticated and expensive simulator of them all was the Waller Trainer. Costing $58,000, it required its own specially built spherical-shaped air-conditioned building. Running simultaneously, five film projectors showed fighters diving at the gunners from different angles on a large screen. Four gunners at a time could be trained in either turrets or flexible mounts. Trainees took aim through their Mk IX gunsights, with an electrical impulse recording their accuracy. A gunshot sound effect registered a hit, while a miss had a more disappointing sound.

Aircraft identification during the early stages of the Pacific War was limited at best. Every radial-engined Japanese fighter was identified simply as a "Zero." As part of his trade, a gunner had to be able to identify both enemy and friendly aircraft in a fraction of a second. Intense study of aircraft identification and recognition was part of the curriculum. Not knowing which theater of operations they would be assigned to, gunners had to memorize aircraft from all the main fighting nations – German, Japanese, Italian, Russian, British, and American. This would be followed by drills. Images would be flashed onto a screen, varying in speed from three seconds to one-tenth of a second, and to pass the final exam students had to correctly identify 100 individual aircraft projected on a screen at 1/25th of a second per type. By late 1943, with the Ki-44 then firmly established in China, it continued to be reported as a "Zero" or sometimes a "Hamp" (the A6M3 Type 32 version of the Zero-sen featuring clipped wings) in most encounters.

After six weeks of training, the graduating

Aircraft recognition during the war was not considered to be of a high standard on either side. American crews identified all enemy single-seat fighters as "Zeros." The vast majority of Japanese fighters used against the B-29 were equipped with radial engines (Ki-43, Ki-44, Ki-84, A6M5/7 Zero-sen, J2M3 Raiden, and N1K2 Shiden-Kai), making recognition difficult when under attack. (Author's Collection)

B-29 SUPERFORTRESS COCKPIT

1. Airspeed indicator
2. Altimeter
3. Bank and turn Indicator
4. Rate-of-climb indicator
5. Magnetic compass
6. Gyro-horizon
7. Pilot direction indicator (PDI)
8. Radio compass
9. Flux gate compass
10. Manifold pressure gauge
11. Tachometers
12. Blind-landing indicator
13. Turret warning lights
14. Bomb release indicator light
15. Vacuum warning light
16. Marker beacon indicator light
17. Alarm bell switch
18. Propeller feathering circuit breakers
19. Breaker reset
20. Propeller feathering buttons
21. Keying button and recognition lights
22. Phone call switch
23. Autopilot controls
24. Bomb salvo switch
25. Formation light rheostat
26. Emergency brake levers
27. Position light switches
28. Landing lights
29. Wing flap switch
30. Landing gear light
31. Propeller speed control
32. Turbo boost switch
33. Circuit breakers
34. Bomb-bay door warning light
35. Bomb-bay door switches and circuit breakers
36. Aisle stand panel light
37. Norden bombsight
38. Control column
39. Rudder pedals
40. Pilot's seat
41. Co-pilot's seat
42. Flap position indicator
43. Propeller rpm limit indicator lights
44. Landing gear indicator lights
45. Bombardier's remote gunsight

gunners received their diplomas and coveted silver wings. Based on test scores, graduates also received arms qualification badges – Expert Aerial Gunner, Aerial Sharpshooter or Aerial Marksman. Upon graduation the new gunners were sent to combat training school. There, for the next three months, they would fly practice missions and hone their gunnery skills.

By war's end American schools had produced more than 297,000 aerial gunners, with those assigned to the B-29 being seen as the cream of the crop. GE's CFC system fitted in the Superfortress was far more complex than a manned Sperry or Martin top turret as installed in other USAAF medium and heavy bombers. It also required a team effort to operate the CFC system effectively, with B-29 gunners being trained as a group and assigned as such. After trainees had completed the normal USAAF aerial gunnery schools, and because of the CFC system's complexity, Training Command accepted only the best for the advanced B-29 gunnery program.

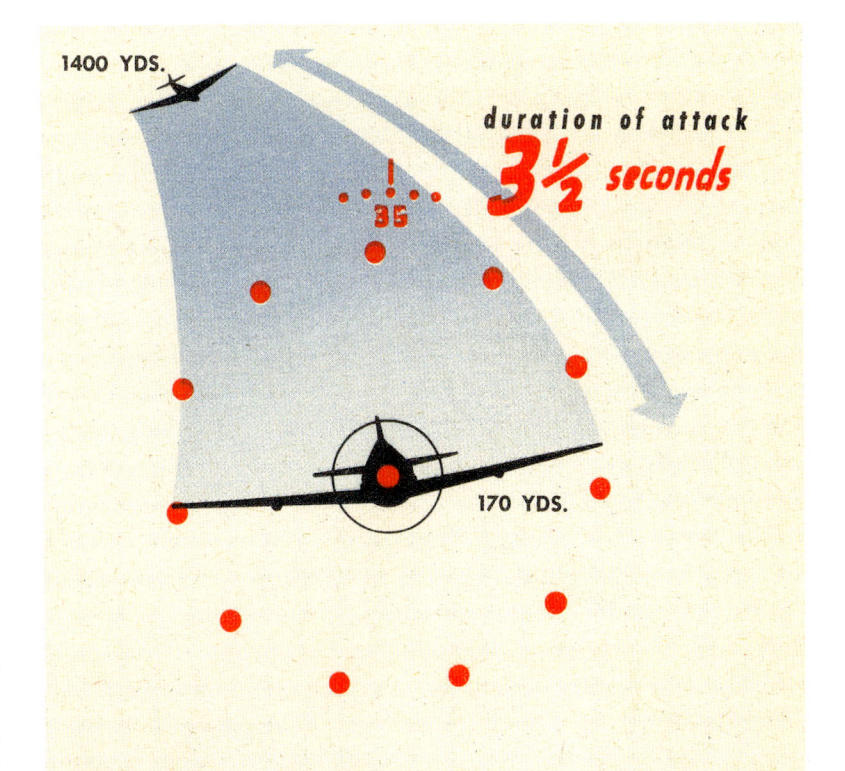

By early 1942 training methods for the advanced Superfortress gunnery system were in development. However, the first training course did not commence until March 1943 when the Power-Operated Gun Turret School opened at Lowry Army Air Field in Denver, Colorado. Conventional training methods used for B-17 or B-24 gunners required modification for B-29 trainees, with the Waller Trainer being adapted for use with remote gun turrets. Initially, future B-29 gunners had to learn their craft in B-17 and B-26 turrets due to a lack of available Superfortresses, however. Later, a handful of Liberators were converted to RB-24L specification, the bombers being equipped with B-29 tail, upper, belly, and chin turrets. The B-29 course was initially 16 weeks in duration, although this was extended to 18 weeks in mid-1944 and to 20 weeks less than a year later. The B-29's CFC system was difficult to master, and with a shortage of Superfortresses for training, the washout rate of 18 percent

ON NOSE ATTACKS open fire at longer range because of the extremely high relative speed between your bomber and the fighter. Fire to kill at 1,400 yards. You will have to be plenty sharp on these attacks because in some cases the relative speed will be as high as 1,000 feet per second. This means that the duration of the attack will only be approximately 3½ seconds. *Brother, think that over!*

Japanese head-on attacks were among the most effective, but most difficult to execute against the B-29. The closing speeds were so high that both the attacking fighter and defending gunner had just seconds to fire at each other. B-29 gunners were instructed to open fire at a range of 1,400 yards. (Author's Collection)

(compared to the 12 percent rate for a conventional gunner) was the norm.

The rush to get the B-29 into combat in 1944 not only revealed a host of mechanical problems, but it also clearly showed that crews were not fully trained. When Maj Gen Curtiss E. LeMay took command of the Twentieth Air Force in China he was so unimpressed with what he found that in September 1944 he stood down his command and sent his crews back to school. By the time LeMay left China in January 1945 he had doubled the B-29's monthly sortie rate, reduced aborts, and raised bomb tonnage dropped on all targets by 250 percent.

For B-29 gunners, their war was far different from their Eighth and Fifteenth Air Force counterparts in Europe. Armed with the most sophisticated remote controlled turret system in the world, they encountered an enemy that was ill-prepared to deal with the fast, high-flying B-29. But even for all its sophistication, the CFC system could not stop determined JAAF and IJNAF fighter pilots from taking their toll. The air battles over Japan also finally laid to rest the concept of the self-defending bomber.

From early March 1945 the majority of B-29 gunners found themselves out of a job. On the night of March 9/10, USAAF strategy in the Pacific war took a new turn when Maj Gen LeMay ordered his Superfortresses to attack Tokyo at night from low-

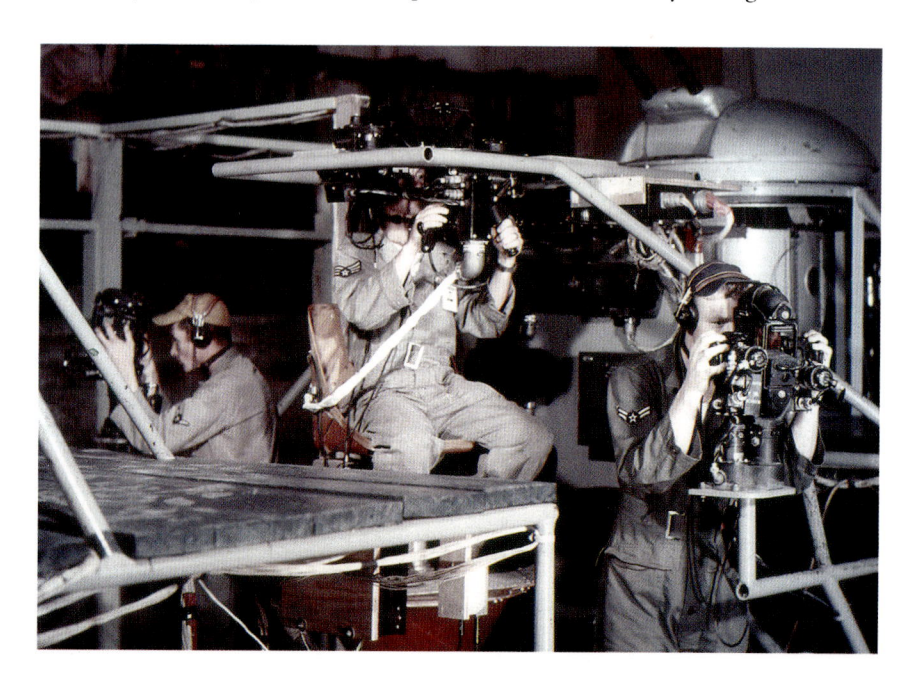

A CFC gunnery commander sits in the "barber's chair." From this position, he has a clear 360-degree view of the airspace above, forward, and to the sides of the bomber. From here, the CFC gunnery commander had sole control of the aft dorsal turret and secondary control of the forward dorsal turret. (National Museum of the USAF)

CFC training schools instructed gunners in teams. Here, three gunners man a GE fire-control CFC simulator. The ring gunner's sight in the center has all the same components and operates in the same way as the pedestal sights manned by the blister gunners. (Author's Collection)

level, with all guns removed except for those fitted to the tail turret. The raid was a major success, making many gunners redundant for the rest of the war. Indeed, the entire 315th BW was equipped with the B-29B, which was armed with just two 0.50-cal machine guns in the tail.

JAAF OPERATIONAL PILOT TRAINING

Throughout Japan's long history, the samurai class held great influence both politically and culturally, and was also well established in the new conscript army. Prior to the war, Japanese education included military drills and martial arts education. Devotion to the Emperor and fulfilling the needs of the state were of paramount importance, subjugating the will of the individual to a group consensus. When JAAF pilots were asked to volunteer for a kamikaze or an air-to-air ramming mission, it was virtually impossible for him to say no. For the individual pilot, peer pressure and perceived group approval were his guiding principles. For a Japanese pilot to question or disobey an order was unthinkable.

JAAF pilot training was also incredibly harsh and brutal, with punishment being an integral part of their training. Physical punishment was common, and no matter how well a trainee performed, training instructors would punish them regardless. By western standards it was completely incomprehensible. Japanese military training focused on total dedication to the Emperor, with a complete disregard for one's self-interest. It also served to instill two main purposes – iron-like discipline and the offensive fighting spirit.

By January 1944 newly trained Japanese fighter pilots faced the same prospect in every theater of operations – more pilots than aircraft. They were also outnumbered, with far less experience and fewer flight hours than their foes. For the novice Ki-44 pilots, it was difficult to gain any combat experience. Pairing a novice pilot with a

The Japanese airfield at Kimpo, Korea, shortly after the Japanese surrender. In the foreground are a number of Tachikawa Ki-55 "Ida" advanced trainers, with Tachikawa Ki-9 "Spruce" and Kokusai Ki-86a "Cypress" biplane trainers lined up behind them. After mastering these types, trainee fighter pilots would move onto the Ki-27 "Nate". By March 1945 all pilot training in the JAAF had come to an end. (National Museum of the USAF)

combat veteran greatly improved the former's chances of surviving his first few missions. However, the reality of combat often meant that seasoned aviators had to abandon their charges to their fate in order to save themselves when engaged by enemy aircraft that were usually more prolific in number, technically more advanced, and flown by better-trained pilots.

By the time the B-29 commenced bombing operations from China in June 1944, the JAAF was in full crisis. The early victories in the first six months of the war had long come to an end. The savage aerial battles over New Guinea and the Solomon islands in 1942–43, sometimes described as the JAAF's "Stalingrad," had cost it hundreds of experienced combat veterans. The slow build-up of Allied air power in the CBI in 1942–44 only added to the relentless attrition inflicted on the JAAF fighter force. As Allied air power increased in volume, the quality and combat effectiveness of the JAAF fighter force began an inexorable decline. Fighting on four fronts – Burma, China, the Southwest Pacific, and the defense of the Home Islands – the JAAF fighter units soon found themselves under strength, under siege, and outnumbered.

The demands for replacement aircraft in all theaters also meant operational pilots were drafted in to ferry aircraft from Japan. During the first half of 1944 the 5th Hikoshidan in Burma received approximately 70 fighters a month – barely enough to cover its losses. The shortage of fuel, combined with the ferry requirement, decimated any time allotted for operational training of new pilots.

Like their IJNAF counterparts, JAAF pilots at the beginning of hostilities were seasoned veterans, many with combat experience gained in China. With war on the horizon the JAAF initiated a rapid expansion of its pilot training in 1941. This was a wise move, but the wartime demand for pilots would prove insatiable. During the first year of the conflict JAAF fighter pilots entered combat with 300–500 hours of flying time in their logbooks. By 1943 those numbers had decreased, with replacement pilots reaching frontline units with 200–300 flying hours, and by 1944 that number had sunk to just 60– 70 hours. The novice pilots would have no real chance of intercepting, let alone attacking, a formation of high-flying B-29s. Their chances of survival were slim and many would perish in operational accidents.

As the number of training hours plummeted large gaps in the hierarchy of skilled pilots quickly appeared. Normally, those with many hours of flying time would serve as flight instructors. By early 1944 such aviators were in short supply. In desperation, many newly graduated student pilots were pressed into service as instructors instead. Fuel shortages also crippled the training cycle. With units being forced to use a fuel mixture of low octane gasoline and alcohol, the number of crashes and deaths only increased.

Up until the end of 1943, however, JAAF pilot training had remained relatively intact. Furthermore, its structure was similar to Allied training programs. A post-war USAAF study detailed the process as follows:

JAAF recruits destined to become pilots passed through the following courses:

Preparatory Training – two to twelve months
Elementary Flying Training – eight months
Advanced Flying Training – four months
Operational Flying Training – two to sixth months

Ki-44-II COCKPIT

1. Army Type 100 reflector gunsight
2. Airspeed indicator
3. Turn and bank indicator
4. Rate of climb indicator
5. Manifold pressure gauge
6. Compass
7. Altimeter
8. Tachometer
9. Fuel pressure gauge
10. Oil pressure gauge
11. Oil temperature gauge
12. Landing gear indicator lights
13. Ho-103 12.7mm machine guns
14. Cabin lamps
15. Elevator trim control
16. Hydraulic pressure gauge
17. Radio tuner
18. Cylinder temperature gauge
19. Exhaust temperature gauge
20. Control column
21. Canopy winding mechanism
22. "Butterfly" flaps control buttons
23. Main switches
24. Oxygen control
25. Oxygen flow meter
26. Fuel gauge (main tanks)
27. Fuel gauge (auxiliary tanks)
28. Left and right auxiliary tank selector
29. Left and right main tank selector
30. Pilot's seat
31. Hydrostatic plunger for main tanks
32. Hydrostatic plunger for auxiliary tank
33. Hydraulic brake pedals
34. Rudder pedals
35. P.4 compass
36. Emergency hydraulic hand pump
37. Magneto switch
38. Throttle lever
39. Mixture control
40. Propeller pitch control
41. Friction adjuster
42. Internal tanks cock
43. Main fuel cock
44. Undercarriage emergency operation
45. Cam manipulation
46. Undercarriage selector
47. Flap selector
48. Compressed air bottle
49. Clock
50. Flap position indicator
51. Hydraulic brake pressure gauge

47

Preparatory Training

The length of this introductory training varies with the age of the recruit. Recruits of military age, and men transferred from other branches of the Army, receive a short two-month "recruit training" course of a general nature, designed to provide an introduction to air force routine and inculcate a spirit of devotion to that service. Boy recruits on the other hand take a 12-month cultural course in academic subjects, including science, languages, arithmetic and history. Physical training forms an important part of the curriculum. Not all graduates of these courses are destined to be pilots.

Elementary Flying Training

Eight months are spent at the elementary flying training schools, during the first six months of which all pilots-to-be train "en bloc" regardless of the type of aircraft they may eventually specialize on. During this period, flying time totals 20 hours dual and 70 solo, a biplane trainer being used. Before the conclusion of the course, recruits are separated into fighter, bomber and reconnaissance classes, and they spend two months converting to the special type of aircraft they will use at the advanced flying training centers. Flying time on this conversion course is reported to be 30 hours.

Advanced Flying Training

Pilots spend four months at an advanced flying training school, where instruction is given in formation flying, combat tactics, air-firing, and night flying. Flying time here is reported to total 120 hours in advanced trainers, obsolescent operational types, and a few first-line aircraft.

Operational Training

Having successfully completed their advanced flying training, pilots are then posted to an operational unit for operational training. This is supposed to last for six months, during which time pilots receive further instruction in combat tactics and become acclimated to local fighting conditions. Although six months is the stated training time, pilots are often required to participate in operations long before that time has expired. Flying times during this stage of training are unknown, though it is believed that efforts are made to raise the trainee's total to 400 hours at least before operations.

These two Ki-44-II Kos were assigned to the Akeno Training Air Division's instructor squad. The aircraft nearest to the camera was manufactured in 1943 with serial number 1200. In the desperate need for more fighters, the Akeno school (along with various other training and testing establishments) was hastily reorganized as a combat unit for the air defense of Japan. In practice these units performed poorly and contributed little, resulting in their disbandment in April 1945. (National Museum of the USAF)

This system was insufficient for the growing needs of the war, and in 1942 it was supplemented by a second system providing additional facilities for advanced flying training. The latter eventually generated three times the number of replacement personnel turned out by the older system. The original training program was maintained, however, as a home organization, with the new syllabus being primarily designed to exploit training facilities overseas, although it was directed from Japan.

In the autumn of 1943, in an effort to increase the flow of pilots, the War Emergency Organization was expanded through the implementation of conscription amongst students in universities and higher schools – classes hitherto exempt from compulsory service. Some 4,000 teaching establishments are said to have been shut down in consequence. This large new influx of recruits was too much for the two existing training organizations to handle, and, consequently, in the spring of 1944, elementary flying training establishments were considerably enlarged and the Advanced Flying Training Regiments were increased in number from 18 to approximately 50. At the same time they were renamed Flying Training Units. Other training units were also formed to conduct specialist advanced flying training.

All these Advanced Flying Training Units (with the exception of about five) were located overseas, being divided, in the second half of 1944, almost equally between Manchuria, Korea, Formosa, the Philippines, Malaya, Java, and China. Their activities were directed, in each area, by Flying Training Brigades, which were in turn subordinated for operations to the Air Army in whose area they were located, and which was responsible for the training in its area.

Fortunately for the Allies, Japanese war planners never prepared for a larger conflict of attrition or for a long defensive battle on multiple fronts. In preparation for war the Imperial Japanese Army established the Army Youth Pilot Program in 1938 in order to build up its strength. Initial intake, however, was just 120 students. American preparations for war were far more ambitious and realistic. With the establishment of the Civilian Pilot Training Program in 1939, the USAAC hoped to produce 20,000 new pilots in the first year alone. Pilot training in the JAAF came to an abrupt halt in April 1945. By the end of the war the USAAF had produced 35,000 fighter pilots. The Japanese managed to produce just 46,000 pilots of all types.

A veteran Ki-43-I Hei is serviced before another training sortie at Narimasu in the fall of 1943. This weary "Oscar" was used as a target tug for Shokis from the 47th Hikō Sentai, a Ki-44-II Otsu of the 3rd Chutai receiving maintenance on its tailwheel behind the Ki-43. (National Museum of the USAF)

Pilots from the 47th Hikō Sentai's 2nd Chutai pose for a photograph on New Year's Day 1944 at Narimasu airfield, near Tokyo. The 47th was brought up to three-chutai strength during the course of that month, the unit being equipped with Ki-44-II Otsus armed with two Ho-301 40mm cannon.

JOHN P. QUINLAN

John P. Quinlan was one of only a handful of aircrew to serve as a tail gunner in both the B-17 and B-29 during World War II. Born in Nepera Park, Yonkers, New York on June 13, 1919, he was known by everyone as "JP." Like tens of thousands of others across the USA on the morning of Monday December 8, 1941, Quinlan was lined up outside his local Recruitment Office (in Buffalo, New York). Tested and deemed fit for the USAAC, he soon made his way to St Louis, Missouri, for basic training. On May 16, 1942 Private First Class Quinlan was promoted to Air Mechanic Second Class. After a six-week gunnery course in Las Vegas, Quinlan was assigned to the B-17-equipped 91st BG and transferred to Walla Walla, Washington, for final training. In July 1942 Quinlan avoided death when his assigned crew undertook a routine flight without him. Their B-17 duly slammed into the side of a mountain, killing all on board. Reassigned to a new crew, Quinlan joined Capt Robert K. Morgan's crew as their tail gunner. Morgan's aircraft was none other than B-17F-10-BO 41-24485 *MEMPHIS BELLE,* which would subsequently gain fame as only the second USAAF heavy bomber to complete 25 missions in the ETO with the Eighth Air Force. It had been assigned to the 91st BG's 324th BS at Dow Field, Bangor, Maine, in September 1942.

Once transferred to England, the 91st went into combat from Bassingbourn, in Cambridgeshire. From November 1942 until May 1943, Quinlan and his crew completed a total of 29 missions, 25 of them in *MEMPHIS BELLE* and the remaining four as a complete crew in other B-17s. Quinlan earned the nickname "Our Lucky Horseshoe" during this period, and he was credited with five German fighters shot down. Having been part of the first crew to complete a 25-mission tour of duty in the ETO, Quinlan returned home in June 1943 with the *MEMPHIS BELLE* for a coast-to-coast 31-city war bond tour. Shortly after returning to the USA Quinlan was given a 30-day leave and was then assigned to the 395th BS/40th BG, which was subsequently equipped with the B-29.

Flying from Chakulia, India, the 40th BG began operations in June 1944. On December 7 Quinlan's luck finally ran out. While flying a mission over Mukden, his aircraft (B-29 42-63363 *Marietta Misfit*) was shot down by flak while bombing the Manchuria Airplane Manufacturing Company. All 11 crew bailed out near Sian, China, Quinlan landing in Japanese-held territory in Manchuria. Although he was soon captured, the veteran tail gunner managed to escape several days later and made his way to Chinese-controlled territory. Eventually meeting up with communist Chinese guerrillas, Quinlan had to fight several pitched battles alongside them before they could take him to a protected landing strip, from where he was rescued. Quinlan subsequently recalled, "They gave me a rifle and I shot at the Japanese soldiers, too. One sees a lot over there that one doesn't want to remember. I'll tell you one thing – those guerrillas were killers. Some of them were only 15 years old, but they had little regard for life."

Finally flown out by a B-25, Quinlan arrived at a nearby airfield still wearing a Chinese guerrilla's uniform. "The crew dropped me off and then quickly departed. The Chinese had given us guerrilla uniforms to wear, and I was standing there in mine when an American officer walked up and asked me to get him some charcoal. He was surprised when I spoke to him in English, explaining that I was an American airman." Quinlan would finish his tour in China with three Japanese fighters shot down, adding to his five in the ETO. He was arguably the most famous, and productive, USAAF tail gunner of World War II.

Honorably discharged in 1945, Quinlan went on to marry and work in construction until his retirement in 1980. He died at the age of 81 in December 2000, being buried with full military honors in the Saratoga National Cemetery in Schuylerville, New York.

Future B-29 gunner Sgt John Quinlan peers out from his tail turret during a break in *MEMPHIS BELLE*'s coast-to-coast 31-city war bond tour in the summer of 1943. (National Museum of the USAF)

MAKOTO OGAWA

Born in 1917 in the Shizuoka Prefecture, Makoto Ogawa joined the 7th Air Regiment at Hamamatsu in 1935. Because of his skill and aggressive flying, he was selected for fighters and graduated from the Kumagaya Aviation School in the 72nd term class in August 1938. Ogawa's abilities as a pilot saw him retained by the school as an instructor, preventing him from being assigned to a frontline unit until he joined the Ki-27-equipped 70th Hikō Sentai in December 1941. From May 1943 the unit re-equipped with the more powerful Ki-44, which it retained until the end of the war. Starting in June 1945, the 70th also began to receive examples of the Ki-84 Hayate, which was one of the best JAAF fighters of the war.

For the first three years of the war the 70th Sentai had been tasked with defending the northern extremities of Manchuria from Anshan. However, in November 1944, with B-29s now attacking the Home Islands from bases in the Mariana Islands, the unit was transferred to Kashiwa as part of the 10th Hikoshidan and ordered to defend Tokyo.

With seven years of flying experience to his name, Ogawa was by then one of the best fighter pilots in the JAAF. His high level of proficiency not only allowed him to battle the B-29 during daylight, but he also quickly developed a method of frontal attack for night operations too. Ogawa's nightfighter method of attack was exceptionally risky. Approaching his target from the frontal quarter and below, he would then rake the belly of an unsuspecting B-29 with deadly 40mm cannon shells. During the infamous night fire-bombing raid on Tokyo on March 9/10, 1945, Ogawa claimed a Superfortress shot down and several more damaged. For daylight missions, Ogawa adopted a more patient method. Only when the B-29s had started to drop their bombs would he attack. Forced to maintain level flight during release, the bomber was an easy target for the skilled Ogawa. Using this method, he was credited with two B-29s shot down.

In one of his most famous combat exploits, Ogawa helped destroy two B-29s with just one firing pass on February 10, 1945 while on patrol over Mt Fuji at 30,000ft. Alerted to an incoming raid, Ogawa and his comrades took advantage of the jet stream winds and raced towards the bombers' target at Ota. He soon caught up with the rear of the 98-strong formation from the 73rd and 313th BWs, diving through the B-29s then zoom-climbing back up at them, firing from below. Setting his sights on a single Superfortress with its bomb-bay doors open, Ogawa fired a short burst. The resulting explosion sent B-29 42-24784 *Slick's Chicks* of the 505th BG careening through the formation, colliding with B-29 42-24815 *Deaner Boy* as it fell away. Both aircraft were destroyed, crashing in Gunma prefecture.

It is not clear if Ogawa's fire alone detonated *Slick's Chicks*' bombs, for while he was attacking from below, 2Lt Toshio Kurai of the 1st Training Unit from Sagami dove at the formation from above. Indeed, he claimed that his victim also collided with another Superfortress. *Slick's Chicks* could also have been hit by flak. Other accounts, however, have Kurai ramming *Slick's Chicks*, causing it to collide with *Deaner Boy*. What actually occurred will never be known. In the end both Ogawa and Kurai were given credit for the bombers' demise – a single B-29 for Ogawa and two for Kurai. For the USAAF, this mission (No. 29) had been the most costly to date – 12 B-29s lost, seven of them ditching. Japanese air defense forces claimed 21 Superfortresses shot down, with the JAAF being credited with 15, the IJNAF three, and three to flak batteries. Seven JAAF pilots had been killed, three of them in ramming attacks.

Ogawa survived the war as the 70th Sentai's top-scoring pilot with seven B-29s and two P-51Ds to his name. On July 9, 1945 he received the Bukosho (instituted by Imperial edict on December 7, 1944, this award was the equivalent of the British Victoria Cross or the American Medal of Honor) and promotion to Second Lieutenant. Post-war, Ogata became a businessman in Tokyo.

B-29 ace and Bukosho recipient WO Makoto Ogawa of the 70th Hikō Sentai is seen here in front of his victory-marked Ki-44. (Yasuho Izawa)

COMBAT

By the time the B-29 finally entered combat with the USAAF, the latter's strategic bombing doctrine had been severely tested. In Europe, unescorted daylight bombing missions had inflicted a heavy toll on both B-17 and B-24 units – between August 1942 and September 1944, the Eighth Air Force alone had lost 3,339 heavy bombers. The concept of self-defending bombers flying in tight combat box formations with massed defensive fire had been clearly disproven. Without long-range fighter escort the Flying Fortresses and Liberators of both the Eighth and Fifteenth Air Forces would have been unable to continue their attacks on heavily defended targets in western Europe.

The B-29 represented the last best hope for the advocates of the self-defending bomber. Because of the aircraft's great range, escort fighters were never part of the equation. With the B-29's advanced CFC turret system, the USAAF believed that the Superfortress would not need any escort. The B-29 also had two other defensive advantages that the B-17 and B-24 lacked – height and speed. While the Superfortress could reach a maximum speed of 358mph at 25,000ft, it usually cruised at 230mph – 48mph faster than the B-17G. B-29s typically flew considerably higher too, often at more than 30,000ft, making it harder for Japanese fighters to intercept them.

Col Paul W. Tibbets, commander of the 509th CG, flew a B-29 without turrets and guns, and he quickly discovered the defensive advantages height allowed. His conclusion about a turretless B-29 was radical, and it did not fit the doctrine at the time:

> By accident I learned that the fighters as we knew them, which included the Jap Zero and the German Messerschmitt, and our P-47s, P-38s and P-51s, could not do any more than make a single pass at the airplane if I could get about another 5,000ft [of altitude] out of

it. How do you get altitude? Sacrifice weight from something else. I had this hulk, this B-29, with nothing [no turrets or armor]. I took that airplane to run the test, and by not paying too much close attention to what I was doing, the airplane kept drifting higher and higher from 25,000ft.

The fighters didn't have enough power and didn't have any maneuverability at 33,000ft. They could get up there, but they were staggering at that point. If they made a pass at us, they stood a chance of scoring a lucky hit, but by the time they could recover [for a second pass], they were so far below us that, [with] the speed of the airplane at that altitude, there was no way they could catch us and climb back up because their engines were overheating.

I think when [Maj Gen Curtiss E.] LeMay first heard about my idea of a bomber without any turrets, he wanted to call the psychiatrist out to have my head examined because the idea in those days was you pile on more armament.

For the CFC gunners, the B-29 was a quantum leap forward. With the aircraft being a more stable gun platform, they were able to open fire at greater ranges. Indeed, gunners could now open fire at a maximum range of 1,500 yards, with an effective range of 900 yards. "Fire range is increased to a point where your fire power is effective beyond the limits of most fighters," noted one B-29 gunner. They also had the luxury of flying in a pressurized environment. Battling sub-zero temperatures and mind-numbing cold for hours on end was now a thing of the past, gunners arriving over the target fresh and ready for action. But even with these many advantages, and improved technology, the B-29 still proved vulnerable to enemy fighters as unforeseen circumstances and changing Japanese tactics quickly eroded the bomber's defensive capabilities.

The B-29's high-altitude performance, while impressive, soon met a new and persistent foe over Japan. In 1944, the term "jet stream" was largely unknown. When

The weather patterns over Japan were hard to forecast accurately and would remain so until the end of the war. Frigid winds from the Asian landmass during winter produced constant walls of cloud off the coast and over the target. (NARA)

first encountered, USAAF intelligence officers were stumped by the howling winds that regularly occurred at high altitude. Clocking in at up to 140mph, these "roaring rivers of air" made combat formation flying impossible, negating the effectiveness of supporting fields of fire. For CFC gunners, the jet stream winds were both a blessing and a curse. Aiming in the turbulent air was far more difficult, but for any attacking Japanese fighter pilots, their ability to intercept and attack individual B-29s became an exercise in futility. This was the first experience of air combat at such heights for either the USAAF or the JAAF/IJNAF, and what the Japanese fighters could not do – disrupt the bombing campaign of the Home Islands – the jet stream winds almost did. Only when the B-29s switched to low-level attacks did the aerial campaign against Japan finally gain momentum.

The first encounter between Japanese fighters and the B-29 occurred on April 26, 1944. Flying supplies over "the Hump" from India to Hsinching, Wichita-built B-29-BW 42-6330 of the 444th BG battled with up to six Ki-43 "Oscars" from the 64th and 204th Hikō Sentais. Capt Hideo Miyabe, commander of the 64th Hikō Sentai, was the first Japanese fighter pilot to attack a Superfortress. B-29 pilot Maj Charles Hanson watched as the six "Oscars" split into two formations of three and took up position on either side of his bomber. For about 15 miles the six Ki-43s kept pace, observing and assessing. Suddenly, the lead fighter flown by Miyabe swung in behind and below the B-29 and opened fire. During the 30-minute engagement the bomber's top turret and 20mm tail guns jammed and side blister gunner Sgt Walter Gilonski was wounded. Towards the end of the engagement tail gunner Sgt Harold Lanahan was able to clear his 0.50-cal machine guns and fire off a number of bursts, claiming one kill.

During the clash Miyabe reported shooting out one of the B-29's right engines. After several passes, and with their fuel now running low, the Japanese pilots finally gave up the attack. Upon returning to base, they claimed to have downed the B-29 – the bomber made it to Hsinching, however, where it was discovered that the aircraft

On November 24, 1944, 111 B-29s from the 73rd BW headed for Tokyo for the first time. Their target was the Nakajima aircraft plant at Musashino, just north of Tokyo. In response pilots of the 47th Hikō Sentai prepare to scramble in their Ki-44-II Heis from Narimasu in the hope of intercepting the high-flying bombers. First blooded in combat over Malaya in 1942, the unit was ordered back to Japan in the fall of 1943. The 47th Hikō Sentai was assigned to the 10th Hikoshidan in defense of the Tokyo area.

had been hit by just eight 12.7mm rounds. According to Japanese records no "Oscars" were lost either.

This attack highlighted a number of deficiencies and common errors committed by both participants that would occur again and again through to war's end. The first was over claiming, which was common on both sides throughout the conflict. Each reported one aircraft shot down, with no real evidence to back up their claims. The B-29, with its formidable armament, suffered a number of failures and was unable to shoot down any of the attacking fighters. Despite making several firing passes, the "Oscars'" weak armament (most likely Ki-43-IIs armed with just two synchronized 12.7mm machine guns) proved unable to dispatch the lone, unescorted, Superfortress.

This came as no great surprise to the Japanese, as Lt Cdr Mitsugu Kofukda of the IJNAF's Sixth Air Corps noted in a post-war report:

> By the time the B-29 Superfortress appeared, we had achieved great strides in increasing the firepower of our fighters and interceptors. However, even these steps came too late, for the B-29 represented a remarkable advance over the tough B-17, and we were unable to keep pace with American engineering developments.

On July 29, 1944, XX Bomber Command dispatched 96 B-29s on mission No. 4 against the Showa steelworks at Anshan, Manchuria. In response, 20 fighters, including five Ki-44s from the 9th Hikō Sentai, were scrambled to intercept the Superfortresses. Already damaged by flak, B-29 42-6274 *Lady Hamilton* from the 468th BG was shot down by the Shokis to give the Ki-44 its first recorded success against the Superfortress. Reacting to the XX Bomber Command raids, the JAAF

The first B-29 brought down during the November 24 raid was Lt Sam Wagner's 42-24622 from the 870th BS/497th BG, their aircraft being rammed by the Ki-44 of Cpl Yoshio Mita from the 47th Hikō Sentai. Lt Wagner is seen here squatting by his dog in the middle of the front row. Only MSgt William Nattrass, standing at the extreme left, survived the attack.

B-29 42-6299 "humpin honey" of the 770th BS/462nd BG was rammed by a Ki-44 flown by either Sgts Tadanori Nagata or Yoshihiro Akeno (both were killed during the mission) from the 104th Hikō Sentai over Mukden, in Manchuria, on December 7, 1944. Only two crewmen from the bomber survived to become PoWs, and they were both released at war's end.

transferred the Ki-44-equipped 70th Hikō Sentai from Japan to Manchuria in August. It was followed by the 104th Hikō Sentai the following month, this unit being equipped with both Ki-43 and Ki-44s at this time.

On September 8, XX Bomber Command launched Mission No. 8, which again targeted the Showa steelworks. The Shokis of the 9th and 70th Sentais intercepted 72 B-29s as they approached their target, pilots from the 9th subsequently claiming five bombers shot down, two probables, and one damaged. The 70th claimed three B-29s destroyed and six damaged. Actual USAAF losses amounted to three bombers, with 42-6234 of the 444th BG being the only bomber to fall to JAAF fighters. B-29 42-6360 of the 462nd BG was written off after it suffered heavy damage belly landing at Lachokow, while 42-6212, from the same group, crashed after running out of fuel.

The first reported, but not confirmed, ramming attack by a Ki-44 also occurred that same day when MSgt Mamoru Taguchi claimed to have rammed his fighter into the tailplane of a B-29 over the Showa steelworks.

On December 7, XX Bomber Command launched mission No. 19, which saw 108 B-29s sent to bomb the Manchuria Airplane Manufacturing Company at Mukden. Some 91 B-29s made it to the target, where they were met by 12 Ki-44s and six Ki-84s from the 104th Hikō Sentai and additional fighters from the 25th and 81st Dokuritsu Chutais (independent squadrons, operating a mix of Ki-45s and Ki-27s). B-29 crews reported 185 single and coordinated attacks by 85 fighters, although the actual number of attacking aircraft was considerably less. Weather over the target was clear, although problems with frosting on the cockpit glass and aiming domes hindered both bombardiers and CFC gunners. The 104th Hikō Sentai claimed six B-29s shot down, including two credited to Sentai CO Maj Yamato Takiyama and MSgt Narimoto flying Ki-44-II Otsus armed with two 40mm cannon. Ramming attacks by Sgt Tadanori Nagata and Yoshihiro Akeno resulted in 42-6299 *"humpin honey"* of the 462nd BG being brought down by Nagata and B-29 42-63355 *Bella Bortion* damaged when Akeno struck the propeller on the No. 1 engine. Both JAAF pilots were killed in action during these attacks.

Mission No. 19 had cost XX Bomber Command seven B-29s (the JAAF claimed 15 destroyed), with operational losses accounting for three of the bombers – the remaining four were either shot down or rammed. JAAF losses were heavy, with five pilots killed and five aircraft (two Ki-44s, one Ki-43, one Ki-45, and one Ki-27) destroyed.

JAPANESE TACTICS

The appearance of the B-29 presented the Japanese with a series of insurmountable problems. During the bomber's early raids, the JAAF had been able to intercept and attack the incoming bombers but had enjoyed only limited success. The small number

Break 1,500ft
457m
(not to scale)

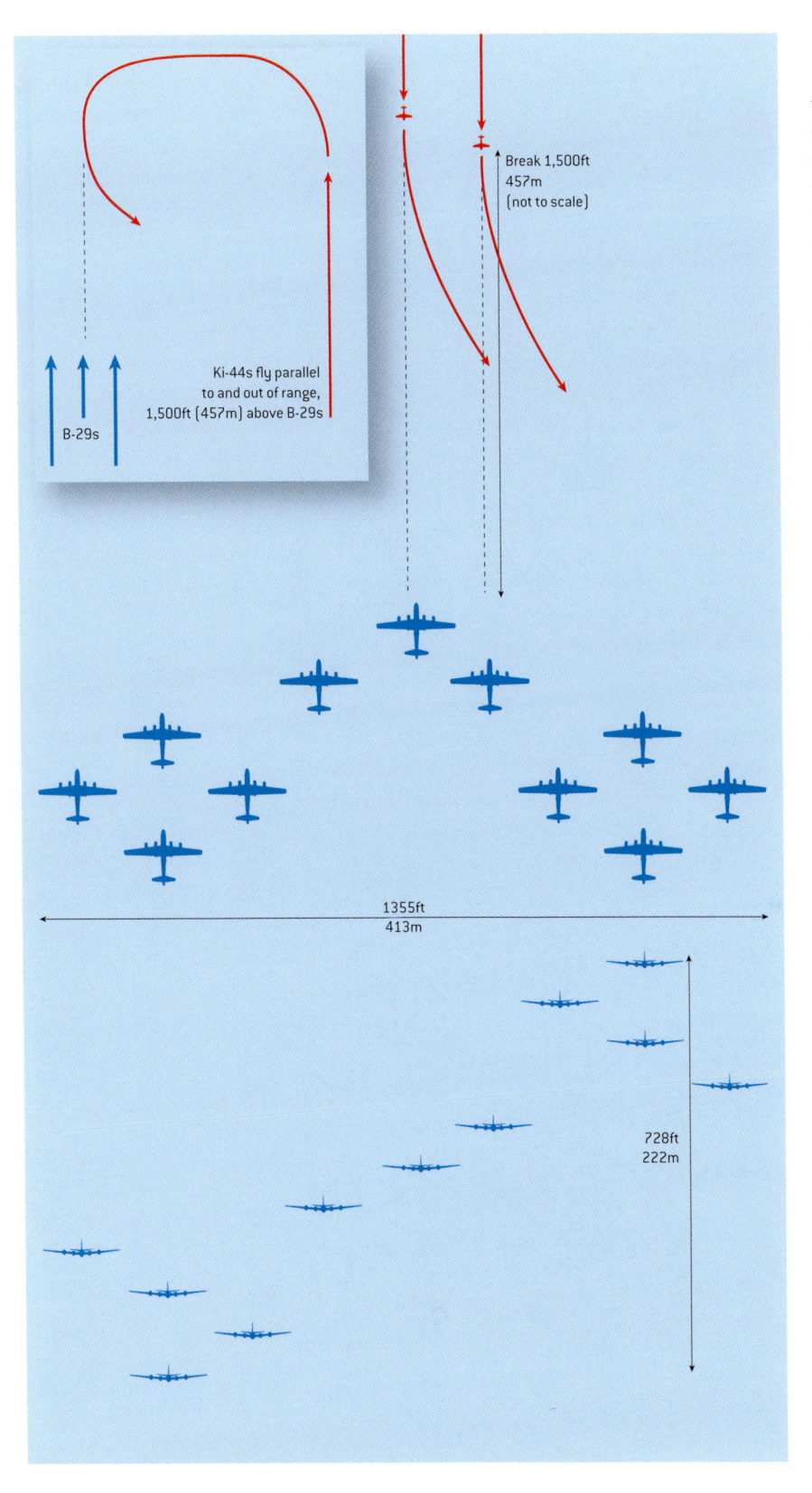

Ki-44s fly parallel to and out of range, 1,500ft (457m) above B-29s

B-29s

1355ft
413m

728ft
222m

The standard B-29 11-aircraft formation, stacked high to the right, was organized in this fashion so as to maximize the effectiveness of the bombers' defensive armament. Each gunner/bombardier was assigned a patch of sky to scan and defend. This reduced fatigue and improved communication between the gunners when under attack. High-altitude winds, however, made tight formation flying such as this difficult, making for less coherent formations and less effective defensive fire. Typically, Japanese air defense fighter units were given, at best, an hour's warning of an incoming B-29 raid. This was barely enough time for a Ki-44 to takeoff from a cold start and reach the bombers' operating altitude of 30,000ft. This meant that Shoki pilots had to be flexible when it came to intercepting B-29 formations. Some were compelled to attack from below, while others were forced to engage the bombers from unfavorable angles and heights. If a Ki-44 pilot managed to climb above the B-29s, it often meant he could make only a single diving pass before suffering an immediate loss of altitude. The head-on attack tactic from slightly above the bomber, depicted here, was thought to be the most effective way to attack the Superfortress due to the vulnerability of its heavily glazed cockpit. It was also the most difficult interception to achieve. Careful coordination and pilot skill was required, for the high closing speeds and light armament of the Ki-44 meant that good marksmanship and a great deal of luck were required if the head-on attack was to be effective.

57

of Ki-44s available, their light armament, and inadequate tactics greatly hindered their success. The scramble to get off the ground and to height meant that there was no time to form up, forcing each pilot to attack individually. CFC gunner Ed Lawson recalled:

> If they had attacked in pairs, as American pilots were taught, we would have really suffered because we could fire at only one plane at a time. Our training was to fire at the closest plane. If the Japanese had come in pairs, the second plane would not have drawn fire.

For Japanese fighter pilots, time was their greatest enemy. Even in the best circumstances with a raid detected inbound from the Marianas at maximum range (by the radar station on Hachijo-jima, a small island due south of Honshu), it took roughly three minutes to assess the enemy's strength and direction and pass the message to Eastern Army Command. Another 20 minutes would usually elapse before the first fighters were scrambled, and the climb to interception altitude took some 50–60 minutes. In the best conditions, it would take more than an hour to reach the incoming raid, making it impossible to reach the B-29s before their bomb run. It also meant some fighters were compelled to attack the Superfortresses from below.

The USAAF soon became fully aware of this, and the following entry from a Tactical Mission Report from 1945 was repeated over and over again:

> Enemy fighter reaction on this mission indicates the continued inability of the enemy to intercept with other than negligible opposition.

In terms of performance, the JAAF considered the Ki-44 to be inferior to the Ki-46 and Ki-61 when it came to high-altitude interceptions, but much better than the obsolete Ki-43 and considerably heavier twin-engined Ki-45.

When photo-reconnaissance optimized F-13A 42-93852 flew over the Japanese capital on November 1, 1944, it was the first American aircraft to do so since the B-25s of the "Doolittle Raiders" in April 1942. Flying at 32,000ft, the lone Superfortress was challenged by Ki-44s from the 47th Hikō Sentai, although it returned to base unharmed. Capt John D. Steakley (far right) was awarded the Distinguished Flying Cross following this mission. Appropriately, his F-13 was christened *TOKYO ROSE* in the wake of this historic flight.

Pilots soon found that the best way to attack a B-29 was from above, but getting into a position to launch such a pass was extremely difficult. The Ki-44's high wing loading meant only one pass was possible at high altitude. Maintaining control at height was difficult, and any slight turn resulted in a dramatic loss of height. Apart from ramming, the best form of attack was head-on. Just as the Jagdwaffe had done during Defence of the Reich missions from late 1942, the Japanese identified the cockpit as extremely vulnerable. Although hitting such a small target at high closing speeds was difficult, a lucky or well-aimed burst into the B-29's cockpit was often fatal.

Although undoubtedly an act of desperation, the concept of ramming was not new to the JAAF. Early in the war Japanese pilots, often with their fighters mortally damaged, would sacrifice themselves by crashing into an Allied bomber. When the B-29s appeared over Manchuria, ramming became a last ditch, but accepted, method of attack. The math was compelling – one fighter for a fully crewed B-29. While crashing a fighter into a target as large as a four-engined bomber seemed simple in principle, the skill required to achieve this successfully, and live, was beyond that of any newly trained pilot. For most unit commanders, the attrition of experienced pilots was not entirely acceptable either.

Nevertheless, in November 1944 the commanding officer of the 10th Air Division ordered all the fighter units under his command to form air-to-air ramming flights. These Shinten Seikutai (Heaven Shaking Air Superiority Units) were equipped with four aircraft each. To improve high-altitude performance, the Ki-44s of the units involved were stripped of armament, protection for their fuel tanks, gunsights, radios, and armor. It was believed that these stripped-down airframes could reach 45,000ft.

By 1944 air-to-air bombing was also an accepted – if somewhat unsuccessful – technique occasionally used by the JAAF to break up enemy bomber formations. Both the 47th and 246th Hikō Sentais equipped some of their Ki-44s with racks to carry the Ta Dan incendiary/fragmentation bombs. In order to have any chance of success the Ki-44 pilots obviously had to be above the B-29 formations – something they were unable to achieve with any regularity. The method was abandoned in early 1945.

Although never intended to fly as nightfighters, 40mm cannon-armed Ki-44s from both the 70th and 246th Hikō Sentais were used in the

Sgt Masami Yuki of the 47th Hikō Sentai rams B-29 42-24655 *Miss Behavin* off the 497th BG over Narimasu on January 9, 1945. Yuki was killed in this attack, his body being found close to the bomber's lost engine. The stricken Superfortress fell out of formation under continuous attack by other 47th Hikō Sentai Shokis led by Capt Yasuro Mazaki, with WO Takashi Awamura also ramming the bomber to finally bring it down into the sea. None of the B-29's crew survived the high-speed ditching. (Yasuho Izawa)

Capt Jun Shimizu led the 1st Chutai of the 47th Hikō Sentai against Capt Steakley's high-flying F-13A on November 1, 1944. All of the Ki-44s he led aloft were fully fueled and armed, which greatly restricted their rate of climb. Hard pressed to reach the 32,000ft mark, Shimizu and his men could only watch in frustration as Steakley's Superfortress flew away. Unable to get any higher, and with almost no control over their fighters, the best Shimizu and his pilots could do was point their noses in the direction of the F-13A and open fire. Shimizu commanded the 1st Chutai from July 1944 through to the end of the war.

59

nocturnal role. Night interceptions took a great deal of skill to execute effectively, and only a small number of aces perfected the art. Nevertheless, operating alone, a handful of pilots achieved some success.

By December 1944 Japanese fighter pilots had gained a good deal of experience intercepting high-flying B-29s. Accustomed to flying in the thin air, they now knew what to expect. Aircraft modifications were also made. The Ki-44s of the 47th Hikō Sentai, for example, had their power increased through the enlargement of the engine's lubricant pipe, allowing more oil to flow around the motor to keep it cool. Ultimately, this all proved to be too little too late.

A Ki-44-II Ko of the 47th Hikō Sentai has its engine run up prior to taking off from Narimasu in 1944. Lacking any wing armament, this aircraft's weaponry is limited to just two fuselage-mounted 7.7mm machine guns. (National Museum of the USAF)

AMERICAN TACTICS

For B-29 aircrews, the Superfortress was a wonder and a curse. Being an immature weapons system, many crews feared it more than enemy fighters and flak. Early high-altitude operations with small bomb loads and poor results offered little satisfaction compared to the risks and the resulting non-combat losses. By March 1945 those worries quickly began to fade, however. On the night of March 9/10, XXI Bomber Command began a series of low-level incendiary attacks that profoundly changed the strategic bombing campaign. These low-level night raids caused massive devastation, providing a degree of battle success proportionate to the effort expended. Morale and fighting spirit rose, as did the reputation of the B-29 as an efficient and reliable aircraft. During one ten-day attack period, 33 crews flew all five missions, while 126 completed four of them.

Every B-29 mission from China or the Marianas to Japan lasted 15 hours and covered more than 3,000 miles. For daylight missions, each Superfortress needed to fly in its assigned combat box formation, although this was tiring and used more fuel. After takeoff, each B-29 flew individually to a designated rendezvous point – for the Guam-based bombers, these took the form of islands off the coast of Japan that had been specially chosen for their easily identifiable characteristics and radar signature. In addition to their primary duties, the left and right CFC gunners acted as spotters, keeping an eye on the troublesome Wright R-3350 engines during the long flights to and from the target. Performing this role took up most of the gunners' time, as according to tail gunner Gene F. Powers of the 9th BG's 5th BS, "The reality was most B-29 gunners never fired a shot in anger."

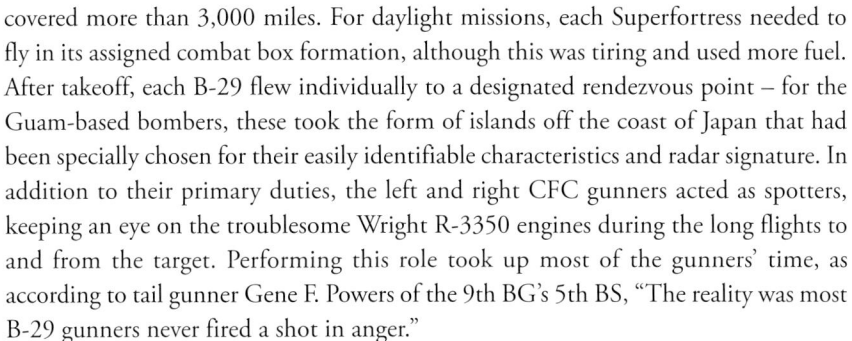

As the B-29s orbited their rendezvous point pilots would search for their correct formation. Formation leaders would identify themselves by lowering their landing gear and/or dropping colored flares. With the aircraft in place, at the appointed time the formation would head to the target regardless of any stragglers – latecomers headed for targets of opportunity or latched onto other formations. Upon entering enemy air space the B-29 would be depressurized (if flying a high-altitude mission) and crews would don their protective gear and oxygen masks. The B-29 combat box was the standard 11-ship stacked high, right formation. Each gunner, bombardier and tail gunner was responsible for a specific patch of sky. Effective communications between all the gunners was essential for mission success and the safety of the other B-29s in the formation. Damage due to friendly fire was not uncommon, as the following extract from a report compiled by the Operational Analysis Section of XX Bomber Command noted on February 10, 1945 when evaluating the combat performance of the CRC system fitted to the B-29:

> There have been 17 instances of self-inflicted damage on Missions 1–25. In practically all cases these were confined to bomb-bay doors, which were riddled on the bomb run.

In an attempt to prevent this from occurring, crewmen were given the following advice in their official Gunners' Information File:

The crew of *Irish Lassie*. In a supreme show of airmanship, pilot Lt Lloyd Avery (standing at far left in the back row) and his crew brought the bomber back to Saipan. Barely under control on final approach, the aircraft smashed onto the runway at 180mph, sending the front wheel slicing through the cockpit floor. Both the tail gunner and radar operator were seriously wounded during the ramming attacks and did not return to action. (Michael Mulligan)

OPPOSITE BOTTOM

On January 27, 1945, during a raid on an engine plant in Musashino, B-29 42-65246 *Irish Lassie* of the 497th BG was attacked by "Tojos," misidentified as Zero-sens – its gunners claimed three of them shot down. Shortly thereafter 42-65246 was rammed by two Ki-61 "Tonys," one of them hitting the left wing behind the outboard engine and the other clipping the left stabilizer. The only known B-29 to survive a ramming attack by two fighters, *Irish Lassie* brought its crew safely home to Isley Field, on Saipan, only to break up on landing. (Michael Mulligan)

WARNING – Always sound a warning over the interphone before you give up control of either or both turrets. If you don't, the gunner who takes over may have his finger on the trigger and the guns will spray bullets into your own formation as they swing into line with his sight.

By February 1945 XX Bomber Command was more than satisfied with the operation and results of its gunners and their powered turrets. "The present armament system has done remarkably well in defending B-29 aircraft of the XX Bomber Command on bombing missions over the Japanese Empire." Up to this point XX Bomber Command gunners had been credited with 123 enemy fighters destroyed, 52 probably destroyed and 179 damaged. B-29 losses due to "action by enemy aircraft" totaled just 24.

Neither XX or XXI Bomber Commands were satisfied with the accuracy achieved by their B-29 crews during early high-altitude attacks, however. Indeed, by February 1945 just one in three bombers sortied on a typical mission was attacking its primary target. The inescapable jet stream winds scattered bombs far and wide, making the doctrinal bombing height of 27,000–30,000ft unsustainable. Some targets had been hit hard, but they were the result of favorable circumstances rather than precision bombing.

To improve results Maj Gen LeMay introduced a new, but proven, tactic – night bombing at low level using incendiaries. Wing commanders were directed to get their groups proficient in low-level night flying. LeMay went a step further by ordering all the defensive armament removed except for the tail guns. On March 9, 1945, 325 B-29s headed for Tokyo. Free from flying in a tight formation, individual B-29s flew as part of a larger bomber stream. Once over the target crews were briefed to drop their incendiary bombs individually within the target area, preferably in spots where fires were not already burning. The raid was a devastating success, with 16 square miles of buildings burned to the ground, 84,000 people killed, and 40,000 injured. Just 14 B-29s were lost to all causes and 40 damaged. Two of the Superfortresses that were shot down fell to Ki-44 pilots. Weaving through the columns of searchlights that night, WO Makoto Ogawa of the 70th Hikō Sentai, flying a Ki-44-II Otsu armed with 40mm wing cannon, claimed one B-29 shot down and several damaged. Fellow 70th Hikō Sentai pilot, and ace,

On January 27, 1945, in one of the bloodiest engagements fought by the 73rd BW, B-29 42-24623 *THUMPER* of the 870th BS/497th BG survived a mass attack by Ki-61s of the 244th Hikō Sentai and Ki-44s of the 47th Hikō Sentai. During the running battle *THUMPER*'s gunners claimed six victories. 42-24623 was one of the first B-29s to return home after completing 40 missions, undertaking a war bond tour.

Capt Yoshio Yoshida also claimed a B-29 destroyed. Post mission reports revealed:

> Enemy air opposition was weak. Seventy-four enemy fighters made 40 attacks. No B-29s were damaged or lost due to enemy action. B-29 gunners made no claims. Surprise was apparently achieved. There was little evidence of air-ground coordination. The enemy pilots intercepting appeared to have little or no knowledge of nightfighting. B-29 crew were able to identify positively only three of the 40 attackers.

For the first time B-29 crews used evasive maneuvers to avoid fighter attack:

> Evasive action (night) was accomplished by some aircraft by making right and left turns and changing altitude. One B-29 changed course, altitude and airspeed to shake off enemy aircraft. One B-29 dived, picked up airspeed and turned. Some aircraft took advantage of clouds to lose enemy fighters, while another B-29 successfully evaded an attack by entering heavy smoke rising from the target.

One of Capt Yoshio Yoshida's aircraft, in this case a Ki-44-II Hei, seen at Kashiwa in June 1945. Yoshida, who claimed six B-29s destroyed, was 1st Chutai leader within the 70th Hikō Sentai, the flash (in red) on the leading edge of the fin signifying his leadership status. Just prior to the end of the war Yoshida underwent a medical examination to check his ability to fly the Mitsubishi Ki-200 Shusui rocket fighter (a copy of the German Me 163). (Yasuho Izawa)

LeMay's gamble had paid off, and it was a major turning point in the strategic bombing campaign against Japan. For the first time since its introduction, the B-29 was now capable of sowing death and destruction on an industrial scale. Operating both day and night, Superfortresses would from now conduct a mix of night incendiary and precision medium-altitude day bombing attacks. As more incendiary raids followed, the JAAF was forced to send an increasing number of its day fighters up at night. For example, on March 16–17, Mission 43 headed to Kobe. As 330 B-29s closed on the target, Ki-44s from the 246th Hikō Sentai rose to the challenge. MSgt Kenji Fujimoto and Sgt Yukio Ikuta both rammed Superfortresses and survived.

For the B-29 crews, Japanese ramming tactics were both terrifying and incomprehensible. For the CFC gunners, it was deeply shocking. To stop a fighter from ramming their aircraft they had to destroy it outright. Ivan Potts, a pilot with the 40th BG, recalled:

> We were flying No. 1 in our formation. The No. 3 plane, which was the one to our right, was deliberately rammed in the back by one of the kamikaze Jap fighters. That was a horrible experience for our crew to see, especially the gunners, right off our wing. I don't think our gunners completely recovered from that for the balance of our missions.

For the Ki-44 pilots, the sudden shift to low-level night attacks changed the nature of the air campaign. Now they had to fight both day and night against an enemy they knew could not be stopped. They also witnessed the wholesale destruction of their cities and homes. Combat was constant, not only against the B-29s but also carrier aircraft that were now marauding over southern Japan with increasing frequency,

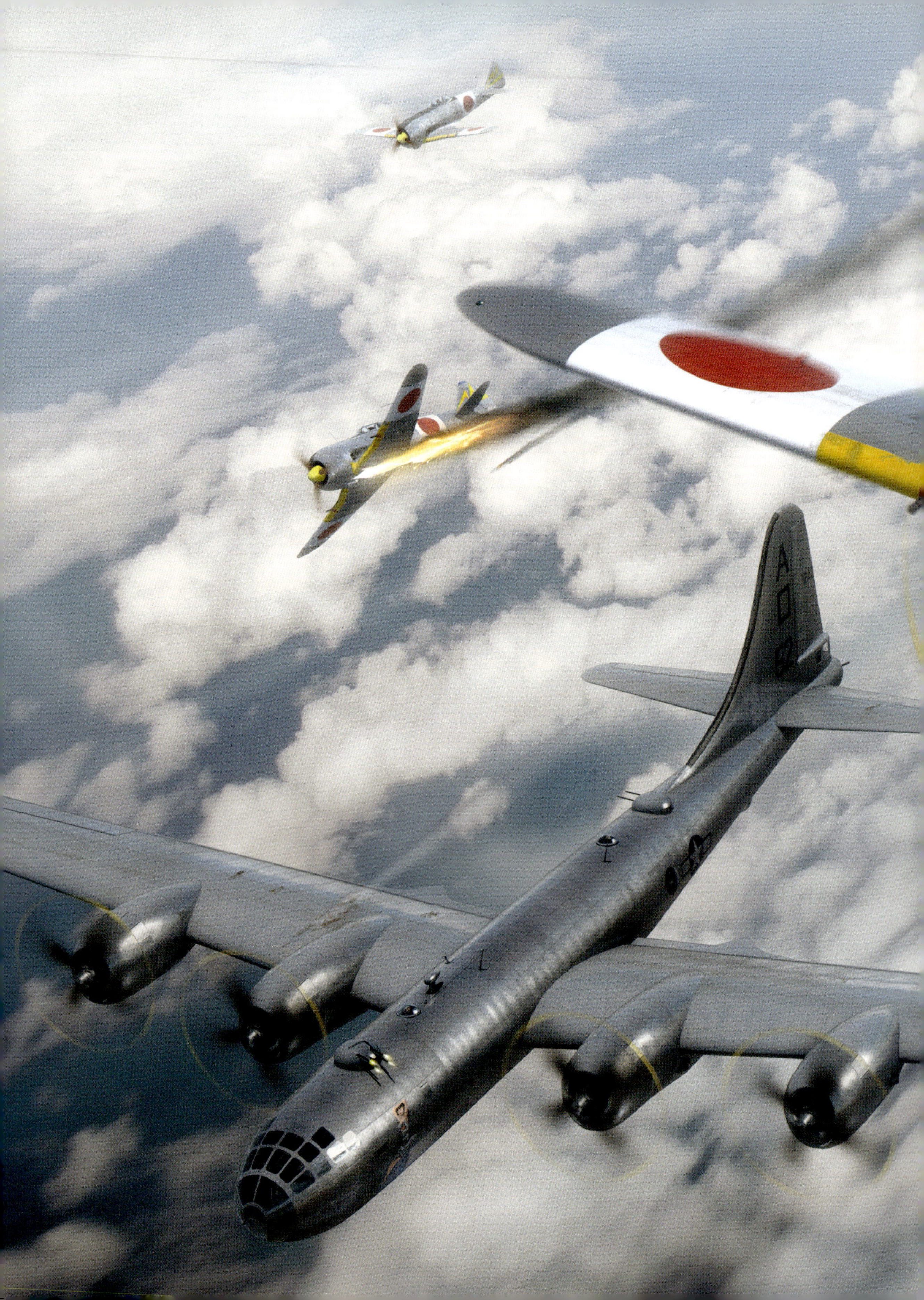

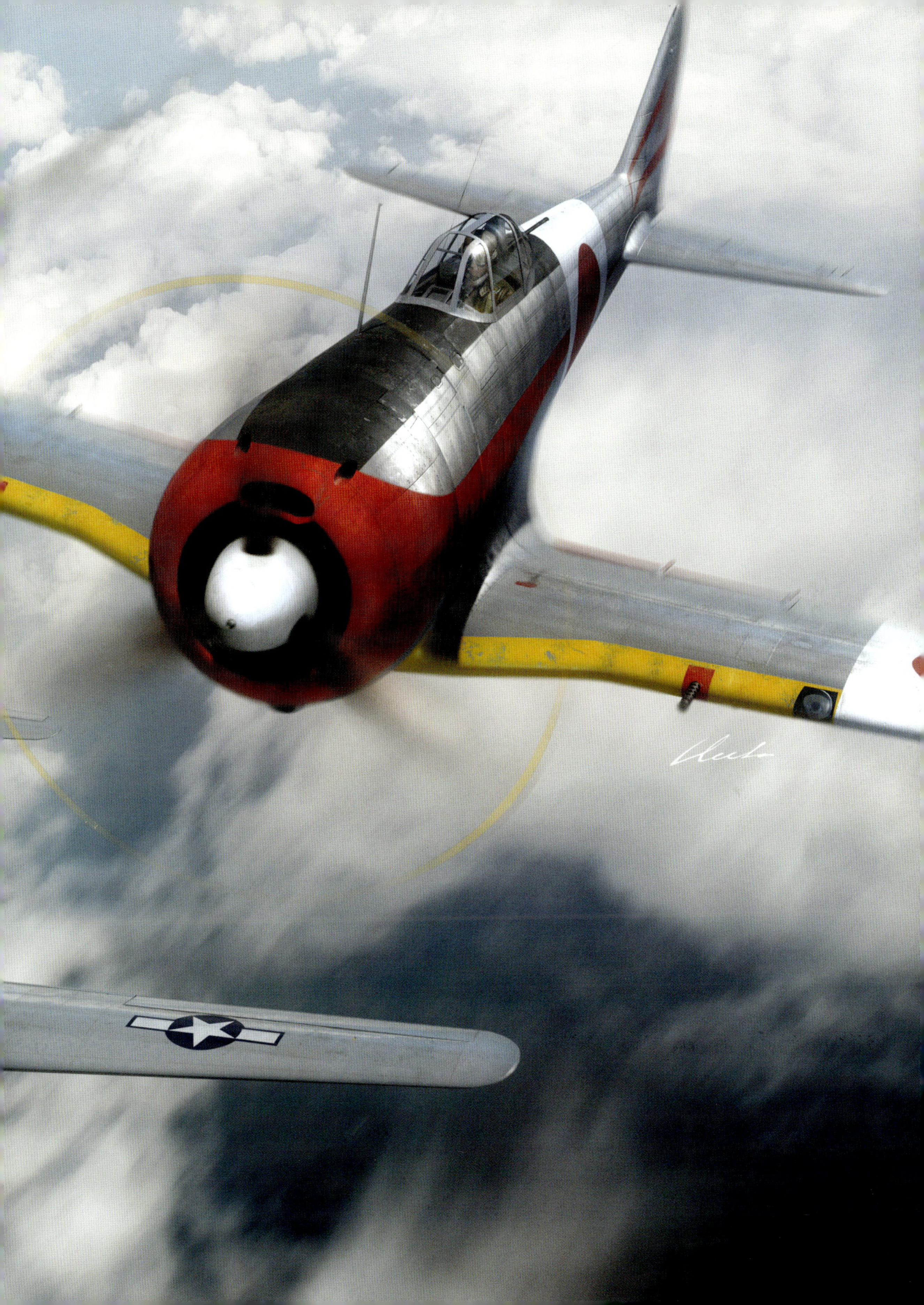

PREVIOUS PAGES
On January 27, 1945 60 B-29s headed for target 357 – the Nakajima aircraft plant at Musashino. Two weather-reconnaissance Superfortresses provided advance information on the conditions over the plant, but by the time the main force reached the target cloud cover had closed in, with a ten-tenths overcast carpeting the area. Unable to bomb the principal target, the main force opted for a radar drop on Tokyo instead. Japanese interceptors reacted with both conventional and ramming attacks, engaging the B-29s between 24,000 and 30,000ft. Bomber crews counted 984 individual attacks.
Leading the mission and taking the brunt of the attack was the 497th BG, with one squadron led by Lt Col Bob Morgan of *MEMPHIS BELLE* fame. Included in the group's formation was Lt Lloyd Avery's 42-65246 *Irish Lassie*, which was repeatedly attacked by a gaggle of Ki-44s from the 47th Hikō Sentai. *Lassie*'s gunners threw up a wall of lead, claiming three Ki-44s (misidentified as Zero-sens) destroyed. But it was not enough. Determined to destroy the B-29, pilots from the 244th Hikō Sentai bored in on the damaged bomber, with one Ki-61 ramming the left wing behind the outboard engine and another clipping the left stabilizer. Nevertheless, *Irish Lassie* miraculously returned to Saipan, where the aircraft was declared a write-off. Its crew had survived, however.

forcing them to engage US Navy Hellcats and Corsairs. Pilot fatigue and the mental strain of combat would have been immense. Air attacks on home airfields only added to the stress, and for some, death by ramming would have been a relief.

To make matters worse still, by early 1945 the decline in flying hours for frontline fighter units was reaching crisis point. Veterans with more than 500 hours and those rated as Class A (fully combat-ready) could be counted on two hands, while nearly half of the pilots in a typical unit had fewer than 200 hours to their names. In sharp contrast, as the B-29 campaign grew in strength, the highly trained CFC gunners were called on to do less. Night missions were flown with just a tail gunner on board, and with Mustangs (and, latterly, Thunderbolts) providing a fighter escort during daylight raids from April 7, 1945, bomber gunners were more passengers than combatants during the final months of the war in the Pacific.

In the spring of 1945 XX Bomber Command completed a study to determine which wounds were directly attributable to enemy weapons. It was determined that approximately 70 percent of all wounds suffered by B-29 crew members were caused by either 20mm shells or anti-aircraft shrapnel, with less than eight percent being attributed to machine gun bullets. Interestingly, approximately 55 percent of all wounds inflicted involved gunners, with about 42 percent of all wounds received being inflicted on the three gunners in the CFC section. It was not fully understood as to why the gunners were more susceptible to injuries than those in other parts of the B-29. This high percentage was difficult to explain considering the fact that the majority of attacks had been high frontal or from the "Eleven" or "One o'clock" positions.

The B-29 also presented a new set of problems for wounded crewmembers. It quickly became apparent that wounds were being inflicted when the aircraft was many hours away from base. Unless quick and effective treatment was applied on the spot, men might die or suffer a severe degree of shock before landing. To address this issue, the USAAF recommended that two enlisted men be given sufficient first aid training that focused on the ability to deal with the suppression of hemorrhages and the administration of morphine and blood plasma. The systematic first aid training of two members of each crew was first incorporated within the 58th BW's Aero Medical Training Program in 1943.

Further improvements to the way the Superfortress waged war occurred in April 1945 when the 315th BW joined XXI Bomber Command. This unit was equipped with the B-29B, which represented a radical departure from the original Superfortress in terms of its armament and precision bombing capability. Equipped with the new AN/APQ-13 Eagle radar system, the B-model allowed the 315th to specialize in nocturnal and bad-weather radar bombing raids. Relying on its speed, the cover of darkness or bad weather, the B-29B was armed with just two 0.50-cal machine guns in the tail. To improve rearward defense, the gunner was equipped with the new AN/APG-15B S-Band Tail Gun Radar system.

April 1945 would also see the first P-51D very long-range escort missions launched from Iwo Jima by VII Fighter Command. On the 7th, the 15th and 21st Fighter Groups escorted 107 B-29s of the 73rd BW when they targeted the Nakajima aircraft factory in Tokyo. Japanese fighters offered stiff resistance over the target, and during 15 minutes of combat the P-51 pilots estimated that 75 to 100 enemy fighters were

ENGAGING THE ENEMY

For Ki-44 pilots, intercepting and shooting down a high-flying B-29 was extremely difficult. By 1944, a small number of Shokis were equipped with the Army Type 100 reflector gunsight. Although a major improvement over the Army Type 89 telescopic sight, it still required the pilot to estimate the angle of deflection to the target. To achieve any degree of accuracy the Ki-44 pilot had to attack at close range from a central position with minimum deflection. And when he did manage to get a B-29 into his sights he only had two or three seconds to deliver an accurate shot.

A further disadvantage was the Shoki's notoriously weak armament. The Ki-44-II Hei was armed with just four 12.7 mm machine guns, two of which were synchronized fire through the propeller. This reduced their rate of fire to 400rpm, compared with 800rpm for the wing guns. A two-second burst would unleash just approximately 42 shells, which was nowhere near enough to down the rugged B-29.

Range estimation was also a serious problem, with most pilots opening fire at 2,000 yards. Attacking a B-29 formation from any angle would attract accurate and deadly fire from its multiple turrets and tail positions. Only the most determined and skilled pilots would close the range and brave the bombers' sustained and coordinated defensive fire. Even when armed with two Ho-301 40mm wing cannon, the Ki-44 was still at a major disadvantage. The heavier weapon's low rate of fire of just 450rpm and a muzzle velocity of 760ft per second meant attacking from point-blank range was the only option. Furthermore, with just ten rounds per Ho-301, the Ki-44 pilot could only fire one or two short bursts.

Pilots of the 246th Hikō Sentai sit ready for action in the winter sunshine at Itami in early 1945. By this late stage in the war the level of experience between JAAF fighter pilots varied greatly. Mixed in with the grizzled veterans would be new pilots and aviators transferred in from floatplanes, dive-bombers or maritime reconnaissance aircraft. Among the seasoned fighter pilots is Sentai commander Maj Kanshi Ishikawa, seated second from the left. (Yasuho Izawa)

seen. Japanese fighter pilots had been advised to avoid combat with the escorting fighters if possible and concentrate on the bombers. However, unable to avoid the powerful escort, the 23rd, 70th, and 246th Hikō Sentais all had Ki-44s shot down. The Mustang pilots claimed 21 fighters overall, for the loss of two P-51s. Three B-29s were also lost, two destroyed by ramming and one by an aerial bomb. By early July 1945 the Mustang units had been joined on B-29 escort missions by three groups equipped with the P-47N. Flying from Saipan, the long-range Thunderbolt would make the skies over Japan even more deadly for the hard-pressed JAAF and IJNAF fighter pilots.

Remarkably, during four months of combat, the Mustangs of VII Fighter Command clashed with Japanese fighters just 15 times over Japan. While Japanese opposition could be fierce and determined at times, the biggest problem the P-51 pilots faced was finding them. Against terrible odds the Ki-44 pilots continued to fight. For example, on the night of May 24/25, XXI Bomber Command suffered its greatest losses during a single mission. Of the 464 B-29s sent to attack Tokyo that night no fewer than 26 failed to return. Five were shot down by fighters, three brought down by flak, one exploded in the air, seven crashed to unknown causes, one ditched, two were listed as missing, and more than 100 were damaged. In exchange, WO Tomoo Yamada of the 23rd Sentai was shot down while hunting over the target area.

On June 5 Kobe was the target for 524 B-29s, of which 494 attacked both it and targets of opportunity. The bombing force went in during daylight and at 18,000ft, losing 11 B-29s to fighters and flak. To the bomber crews the fighter attacks were as vicious and relentless as ever, combining gunnery runs and ramming attacks. 40th BG pilot Ivan Potts described an attack by a 40mm-armed Ki-44-II Otsu (identified erroneously as an IJNAF Kawanishi N1K2 "George"):

> The thing I remember most of all was this ["Tojo"] fighter. As we were coming in on the target we were flying lead airplane in the right hand flight of the lead flight, and we could see this ["Tojo"] circling around down below us. All at once he decided to make his move. He pulled up and he circled around in front of us, and you could almost tell that he had picked us out. As he came in level against us he rolled that baby over with that big round group of cylinders on this thing that reminded me of an old Gee Bee sportster like Col Roscoe Turner used to fly back in the "thirties."

It was a beautiful day – it was as clear as could be. He was out several hundred yards, and he headed right in our direction, closing on us at a tremendous rate of speed. He rolled that ["Tojo"] onto its back and fired two 40mm cannons at us and headed straight down. All the time our new bombardier was pointing and saying "Look at him come," and, as I remember I said, "Look at him? Hell – shoot, shoot!" but nothing ever happened. I don't think we got a shot at him from the nose.

One of the cannon shells hit our left outboard engine. It was a monstrous shell and that engine went out immediately – we were able to feather it. The other shell hit us absolutely in the middle of the bomb-bay. This was only about 15 or 20 seconds after the bombs had gone. Later on our groundcrew told us that they counted 148 holes in the bomb-bay of the airplane. And, of course, we really figured we were in trouble at that time. We didn't know whether we were going down, whether we were going be able to keep that baby up there, or just what in the world was going to happen.

Potts and his crew managed to get back to Iwo Jima, where they crash-landed. Of the 11 B-29s lost over Japan that day, one was rammed and three were shot down by fighters.

A force of 510 Superfortresses targeted Osaka and a number of industrial targets on June 26, and 24 Ki-44s and Ki-84s of the 246th Hikō Sentai, led by sentai commander Maj Kanshi Ishikawa, were scrambled to challenge them. Three B-29s were claimed for the loss of three pilots, including the 1st Chutai leader Capt Sadahiko Otonari, who rammed one of the bombers and died in the collision. Otonari was credited with four B-29s destroyed and eight probables. His wingman, Sgt Minori Hara, was also killed.

On July 1 the Imperial General Headquarters attempted to simplify the air defense structure by placing the 10th, 11th, and 12th Air Divisions under the direct control of the Air General Army. Rather than tying all defending air units to strategic locations, they were formed into Air Defense Duty Units to provide both permanent and mobile forces that could be used to concentrate strength against major threats. The permanent forces were to be provided by four fighter regiments in the Eastern District, four regiments in the Tokai and Central Districts, and one to three fighter regiments in the Western District. As part of this plan,

B-29 42-65296 *The Ancient Mariner* of the 883rd BS/500th BG unloads seven 2,000lb AN-M66 general purpose demolition bombs. The AN-M66 weapon was almost always used against reinforced structures. Assigned to the 883rd BS in early January 1945, 42-65296 had flown 52 missions by the time it was returned to the USA shortly after VJ-Day. (Warren Thompson)

A trio of 70th Hikō Sentai Ki-44-II Heis are run up by mechanics using a Toyota KC truck. The latter had a power take-off driving a shaft above the cab that was connected to the lug on the spinner in order to start the engine. These vehicles were used to start many different JAAF aircraft types, and they were a common sight on airfields. Aircraft "12" and "63" show evidence of former ownership by the 47th Hikō Sentai, having probably been relinquished when that unit began to re-equip with the Ki-84 Hayate. (National Museum of the USAF)

"Sei-Go" (the 20th Fighter Group) was formed from the Akeno and Hitachi Air Training Divisions in the Tokai area as part of the mobile reserve.

The permanently stationed air defense forces deployed two Ki-44 hikō sentais within the Eastern District's 10th Air Division, namely the 23rd (20 fighters) at Imba and the 70th (29 fighters) at Kashiwa, and one Ki-44 hikō sentai, the 246th (18 fighters) at Taisho within the Central District's 11th Air Division. These were the last dedicated Ki-44 fighter units to defend Japan, and they constituted almost 31 percent of the permanently stationed force, thus demonstrating that the type would continue to be an integral part of the air defense of Japan to the very end.

The other permanently stationed defense fighter types were the Ki-45 "Nick" and interceptor versions of the Ki-46 (25 percent), the Ki-61 "Tony" (29 percent), and the Ki-100 – the accidental but excellent radial-engined Ki-61 hybrid (15 percent). The mobile air defense forces were equipped exclusively with the Ki-84 Hayate (66.5 percent) and the Ki-100 (33.5 percent). By this time the veteran 47th Hikō Sentai, forming the mobile 30th Air Fighter Group in the Western District, together with the Ki-61/Ki-100-equipped 244th Hikō Sentai, had re-equipped entirely with the Ki-84.

Taking the air defense force as a whole, therefore, the Ki-44 still represented 18 percent of JAAF's fighter air power – a tribute to the longevity and usefulness of a type that only represented nine percent of total fighter production, and whose production had ceased in January 1945.

After this re-organization, the Ki-44 continued to fly and fight against the Superfortress, as well as the Mustang, Thunderbolt, Hellcat, and Corsair, its pilots believing that the final battle for the homeland was imminent, but with no idea that a single B-29 would change things forever. The last combat casualty for the 70th Hikō Sentai occurred on August 10 over Tokyo when Capt Kanji Honda (the 1st Chutai leader) was killed in a clash with long-range Mustangs of the 15th and 506th FGs. The last major fight for the 246th Hikō Sentai came on the 14th when four Ki-44s took on a force of Mustangs, claiming one but losing Sgt Maj Kenji Fujimoto in return.

The following day Japan surrendered.

STATISTICS AND ANALYSIS

"Control of the guns was not entirely by one person. The control could be swapped around depending on which gunner had the best view, so, it really was not possible to figure out who had been firing."
Edwin Lawson, CFC Ring Gunner, 500th BG

During the last eight weeks of the war, B-29 strength in the Pacific more than doubled. It was an awesome display of air power, and one the Japanese were never fully prepared for or completely understood. For nearly two years after the "Doolittle Raid," the development of an effective air defense system was given a low priority. Inter-service rivalry posed the greatest threat, with a post-war US Bombing Survey concluding that "there was no efficient pooling of resources of the Army and Navy. Responsibility between the two services was divided in a completely impractical fashion, with the Navy covering all ocean areas and naval targets, and the Army everything else."

As a perfect example of how the Japanese military wasted their modest resources during the ill-fated defense of the Home Islands, both the IJNAF and the JAAF established separate radar warning systems. Sixty-three early warning sites were built, 37 by the IJNAF and 26 by the JAAF. Both forces made use of the NEC Type B early warning radar, later called the Tachi-6 in its fixed version and Tachi-7 in mobile form. About 825 sets were built for both forces, but the radar's short range of 155–190 miles and its inability to distinguish between a flight of B-29s or P-51s made it a poor performer. Fortunately for the B-29 crews, the Japanese tended to squander their limited assets through duplication, often locating IJNAF and JAAF radars side-by-side at the same location! Japanese radar was rated as "very poor" by Allied standards and fighter direction remained primitive as a result. Furthermore, radar sites and radio communications between fighter directors on the ground and pilots attempting to intercept B-29s were easily jammed by American electronic countermeasures.

For the Japanese home defense fighter pilots, their minimum objective was to shoot down at least half of any attacking bomber force. Their efforts, however, were spectacularly ineffective primarily due to their paucity in numbers. From July 1944 through to August 1945, home defense fighter strength averaged just 400 aircraft. Only in April 1945 did that number rise above 450, although poor serviceability rates would have meant that most of these aircraft would have remained firmly on the ground. During the B-29's 15-month campaign more than 31,300 sorties were flown over the Home Islands, yet only 74 B-29s were shot down by enemy fighters and perhaps 20 more fell due to a combination of fighters and flak. Some Japanese sources list 142 B-29s as having crashed on Japanese soil or in the "nearby sea." This loss rate was just 0.24 percent of effective B-29 sorties. When one considers that the USAAF's Eighth Air Force lost more bombers to Luftwaffe fighters and flak in one month than the total Superfortress losses in 15 months, the B-29 crews had it easy. That low loss rate, however, came at a high price.

In strictly combat loss terms, the numbers were indeed low, but the overall loss of B-29s to all causes was far higher. Of the 414 aircraft that were destroyed, 148 were attributed to fighters, flak, and ramming attacks, 151 to operational causes, and 115 were classified as "unknown" – the latter were most likely brought down as a result of battle damage. Training accidents alone accounted for more B-29s lost than were shot down over Japan – 97 in-theater. No fewer than 3,111 Superfortresses were damaged, 419 of them seriously.

Without the island of Iwo Jima, B-29 losses would have been much higher. Seized by the US Marine Corps at great cost by late March 1945, it quickly became a life saver for Marianas-based B-29 crews. By war's end 2,251 B-29s had made emergency landings there. Many never made it back into the air, some 286 Superfortresses being scrapped/cannibalized there due to battle damage. While Iwo Jima kept B-29 loss rates low, the cruel trade off came at the price of 6,821 dead Marines and more than 19,000 wounded (almost 18,500 Japanese soldiers were also killed). The Battle of Iwo Jima would see US forces suffer their highest casualty rate of the 20th century.

VII Fighter Command would count 91 pilots lost to all causes while flying escort and fighter attacks over Japan. B-29 aircrew losses in action amounted to 1,090 killed, 1,732 missing in action, and 362 returned prisoners of war.

The B-29 was the first bomber to fly transoceanic combat missions. Up until November 1944 XX Bomber Command's raids had included a 600-mile overwater crossing from the Chinese coast to the southern Japanese island of Kyushu. Missions from the Marianas were even longer – 1,500 miles one way – a roughly 15-hour round trip, the majority over water. In many ways the vast expanse of the Pacific Ocean between the Marianas and Japan was

A left side blister CFC gunner poses for the camera. In the combat zone the B-29 would be depressurized, forcing all crew members to wear their oxygen masks. (National Museum of the USAF)

a more formidable enemy than the IJNAF and the JAAF. Flying over the northern Pacific, crews that were lost, damaged or short on fuel faced two options – ditch or bale out. Even in the best of sea states, finding a small yellow raft in a vast blue expanse was nearly impossible, but miraculously it was done on numerous occasions.

When sorties began from the Marianas, the responsibility for ASR was originally assigned to the theater commander. It was also a divided responsibility between the USAAF and the US Navy. Between November 1944 and March 1945 48 Marianas-based B-29s, with a total of 528 crew onboard, ditched. Only 164 of them were located and retrieved, which meant that fewer than one in three was rescued. By the end of May the situation had improved greatly, with eight in ten fliers being plucked from the sea. Overall, 654 of the 1,310 aircrew that were forced to ditch or bail out over the sea were saved – of that number, half were B-29 crewmen. By June 1945 the ASR forces were impressive, with 14 submarines, 21 flying-boats, nine super-dumbo aircraft (B-17s and some B-29s equipped with an "air-dropable" lifeboat), and five ships capable of being deployed.

During raids on Japan the USAAF counted 11,206 fighter attacks against the B-29. CFC and tail gunners claimed 914 fighters shot down, 456 probably destroyed and 770 damaged. Although these were impressive numbers, they were grossly overstated. Overclaiming on both sides was common. An extreme example of this occurred in November 1944 when eight B-29s from the 40th BG's 45th BS targeted the Nippon air depot at Mukden, the bombers being attacked by a single Ki-27 "Nate" as they neared the target. The official mission summary that was subsequently compiled noted that the enemy aircraft had been sighted by 17 gunners and bombardiers, all of whom claimed they had shot it down!

The speed and confusion of battle often meant multiple gunners from the same aircraft, or several other bombers in the formation, could have shot at the same aircraft. Although confirming which gunner actually shot down a diving fighter often proved to be an impossible task, it cannot be denied that the Japanese paid a heavy price when trying to engage formations of B-29s. IJNAF and JAAF records note that more than 4,200 fighters were lost over Japan during World War II, 1,450 of them in combat and 2,750 to non-combat causes.

Japanese claims for B-29s shot down were equally distorted, with JAAF pilots stating that they destroyed at least 470. Fourteen Ki-44 pilots were credited with one or more B-29s shot down, and like Superfortress gunners, the numbers they claimed are by no means definitive. The JAAF did not recognize individuals as aces, attributing victories to the unit instead. In total the top Ki-44 pilots claimed 60 B-29s shot down between them. This was an impressive tally when one considers that the Ki-44 made

Capt Yoshio Yoshida was one of the leading B-29 aces of the 70th Hikō Sentai. All his confirmed Superfortress victories were scored at night, and he is seen here standing in front of a Ki-44 elaborately marked with each of his victories. In the JAAF, successful night interception sorties were considered the mark of an exceptionally skilled fighter pilot.

JAAF Ki-44 B-29 KILLERS		
Pilot	Unit	B-29 Claims
Kensui Kono	70th Hikō Sentai	9
Makoto Ogawa	70th Hikō Sentai	7
Yoshio Yoshida	9th Hikō Sentai	6
Yoshio Yasuda	various	6 (10 victories in total)
Akira Kawakita	9th Hikō Sentai	5
Sadahiko Otonari	246th Hikō Sentai	4
Yasuhiko Kuroe	various	4 (51 victories in total)
Heikichi Yoshizawa	47th Hikō Sentai	4
Kenji Fujimoto	246th Hikō Sentai	3
Tomokitsu Yamada	23rd Hikō Sentai	3
Atsuyuki Sakato	70th Hikō Sentai	3
Kiyoshi Otaki	70th Hikō Sentai	3
Yamato Takiyama	104th Hikō Sentai	2 (9 victories in total
Yoshio Hirose	various	1 (9 victories in total)

up just 18 percent of the JAAF's defensive fighter force. The high-scoring aces included Capt Yoshio Yoshida of the 70th Hikō Sentai, who was credited with six B-29s at night, and Capt Kensui Kono, from the same unit, who was the ranking Shoki ace in terms of Superfortress victories, with nine bombers destroyed.

A fighter is only as good as the men maintaining and flying it. World War II fighters are usually measured as good or bad in terms of speed, rate of climb, and firepower. Taken alone, these numbers might be impressive, but a fighter's true effectiveness can only be measured by how well it performs when committed to combat in numbers. The Ki-44 was an average to good fighter in terms of performance. However, the aircraft's effectiveness in action was limited due to a small production run, inadequate armament, low serviceability rates, and a lack of well-trained pilots to fly it. Furthermore, Nakajima's inability to improve the Shoki's high-altitude performance made it a poor performer against the B-29. Simple modifications like a two stage two-speed supercharger, higher octane fuel, and improved armament of four 20mm cannon could possibly have improved the chances of Ki-44 pilots downing more B-29s than they did. The fact still remains though that the JAAF never had enough aircraft, or pilots to fly them, to create an effective fighter force in 1944/45.

Despite the JAAF and IJNAF having had four years to study the air war over Europe and prepare for what was to come, the defenses they put in place would prove shockingly inadequate when it came to repelling attacks on the Home Islands. Instead of pulling most of their fighters from other theaters of war to help defend Japan, neither the JAAF or the IJNAF ever had more than 26 percent of their total fighter force assigned to homeland defense. At the beginning of September 1944, for example, the JAAF had between 30 and 40 percent of its fighters based in the Philippines, with the rest flying from airfields in the China, Burma, and Southeast Asian theaters.

AFTERMATH

The B-29 will be forever remembered as the world's first atomic bomber. On August 6, 1945, B-29 44-86292 *ENOLA GAY* of the 509th CG dropped the first atom bomb, codenamed "Little Boy," on Hiroshima. The results were unprecedented. No fewer than 70,000 people were killed outright, while 60,000 buildings were completely destroyed. Three days later, B-29 44-27297 *BOCKSCAR*, carrying the "Fat Man" plutonium weapon, laid waste to Nagasaki. This bomb destroyed approximately 60 percent of the city and killed 35,000 people. On August 15 the Japanese finally capitulated.

Although surrender may have brought peace, the B-29s continued to fly. Finding and locating PoW camps in China, Japan, and Korea quickly became a top priority. Once these had been located, the Twentieth Air Force

A Ki-44-II Hei – most likely from the 70th Hikō Sentai – sits in a purpose-built revetment at Kashiwa, on the outskirts of Tokyo, in the spring of 1945. The muzzles of the wing-mounted Ho-103 12.7mm guns are covered by protective fairings. (National Museum of the USAF)

Captured Ki-44s of the 9th Hikō Sentai were briefly inducted into Nationalist Chinese (Kuomintang) service alongside other ex-Japanese aircraft within the 6th Fighter Bomber Group. 9th Hikō Sentai ace Yoshitaro Yoshioka remained in China to train Chinese student pilots on how to fly the Ki-84, but there is little evidence for their use in combat during the civil war. Parked behind this weary Ki-44 are two Ki-9 "Spruce" biplane trainers. (National Museum of the USAF)

assumed responsibility for air-dropping supplies to 154 of the known camps in August and September. Specially modified B-29s soon began parachuting in emergency packages that contained food for three days, plus clothing and medical kits. For three weeks, Superfortresses flew almost 1,000 mercy sorties, dropping nearly 4,500 tons of supplies to approximately 63,500 prisoners. It was an amazing feat, but it came at a cost – eight B-29s crashed, killing 79 airmen.

At war's end, Japanese forces occupied a wide swath of territory. According to the US Strategic Bombing Survey there were a reported 1,000 Japanese aircraft in Southeast Asia alone. There was also an unspecified number in China, Manchuria, and Korea that went unreported. Many of the serviceable aircraft left behind were quickly made operational by the newly formed post-war governments. One of the most powerful of these was the Communist Chinese Air Force (CCAF). For the first time in its history the communist Chinese possessed a modern air force, but they did not know how to use it. The CCAF's fighter force consisted of a good number of Ki-43s and Ki-84s, as well as a handful of Ki-44s. Many of the displaced Japanese pilots and mechanics signed up as mercenaries with the communist Chinese, making the new CCAF the most powerful in northern China. The Nationalist Chinese also made limited use of the abandoned Japanese aircraft, as they also took charge of similar equipment to that which had been turned over to the communists. For example, the Ki-44s of the 9th Hikō Sentai at Nanking were taken on charge and pressed into service.

Originally conceived for the heavy fighter-versus-fighter role, the Ki-44 would go on to fill many different roles including bomber interceptor, air superiority fighter, ramming fighter, and nightfighter. Overshadowed by the more famous A6M Zero-sen (in both the fighter role and kamikaze) and the numerically superior Ki-43 "Oscar," the Ki-44 has never been viewed as one of the great fighters of World War II. Its limited production run of 1,225 examples represented just nine percent of the JAAF single-seat fighter production, limiting its use and effectiveness.

The B-29 would be one of a handful of World War II aircraft to see action in two conflicts. On June 25, 1950 North Korean troops crossed the 38th Parallel into South Korea, thus starting the Korean War. At the time the Far East Air Force (FEAF) was equipped with 22 B-29s (many were World War II veterans), 24 weather reconnaissance WB-29s, six reconnaissance RB-29s, and four ASR SB-29s. It was over Korea that CFC gunners would encounter a new and far deadlier enemy than the Ki-44. In the late fall of 1950 the swept-wing MiG-15 jet fighter appeared in the skies over North Korea. The number of communist jet fighters steadily increased through 1951, and on October 23 that year eight B-29s from the 307th BG encountered more than 50 MiG-15s. Out-gunned and out-ranged, three B-29s were shot down and five badly damaged. The MiG-15 was proving to be a tough adversary, with the bomber's 0.50-cal machine guns being considered "worthless" against it. Shortly after this mauling the B-29 returned to its more familiar role as a night bomber, relying on the cover of darkness to help shield it from marauding, but radarless, MiG-15s.

CFC gunners would be credited with 16 MiG-15s shot down, but like the claims made in World War II, this figure was highly inflated. Indeed, many gunners believed they never hit a thing when trying to defend their aircraft from jet fighter attack.

The B-29's war in Korea ended in July 1953. After three years of conflict, Superfortresses from the FEAF and Strategic Air Command (SAC) had flown more than 21,000 sorties and dropped nearly 167,000 tons of bombs. A total of 34 B-29s had been lost in combat, 16 to fighters, four to flak, and 14 to other causes.

Construction of the B-29 ended in May 1946, with the last example rolling off Boeing's Renton production line on the 28th of that month. Hundreds of new and combat-weary examples were put into storage, many of which would eventually be returned to service during the Korean War. As part of the Mutual Defense Assistance Program (MDAP), the Royal Air Force also received 84 B-29As and three B-29s between 1950 and 1952. Given the name Washington, none of these aircraft were nuclear capable. They would serve in the bomber role with the RAF until 1954, when they were returned to the USA.

When SAC formed on March 21, 1946 the small number of *Silverplate* B-29s assigned to the 509th CG were the only nuclear bombers in the world (at that point the USAAF had nine nuclear weapons and 27 B-29s capable of delivering them). They would retain this distinction until replaced by the Convair B-36 Peacemaker in the summer of 1948.

The blackened exterior of this 19th BG B-29 gives it an ominous appearance. The group was based at Kadena air base, on Okinawa, during the Korean War, its trio of squadrons (28th, 30th, and 93rd) being immediately thrown into action attacking invading North Korean troops and other targets from June 28, 1950. By war's end three years later the 19th had completed almost 650 combat missions. (National Museum of the USAF)

FURTHER READING

BOOKS

Anderton, David A., *B-29 Superfortress at War* (Scribner, 1978)
Birdsall, Steve, *Saga of the Supefortress* (Doubleday, 1980)
Bodie, Warren M. and Ethell, Jeffrey L., *World War II Pacific War Eagles in Original Color* (Widewing Publications, 1997)
Bowman, Martin W., *USAAF Handbook 1939–1945* (Stackpole Books, 1997)
Dick, Ron and Patterson, Dan, *American Eagles – A History of the United States Air Force* (Howell Press, 1997)
Dorr, Robert F., *Osprey Combat Aircraft 33 – B-29 Superfortress Units of World War 2* (Osprey Publishing, 2002)
Dorr, Robert F., *Osprey Combat Aircraft 42 – B-29 Superfortress Units of the Korean War* (Osprey Publishing, 2003)
Doty, Andy, *Backwards into Battle* (Tall Tree Press, 1995)
Ethell, Jeffrey L., *How to Fly the B-29 Superfortress – The Official Manual for the Plane that Bombed Hiroshima and Nagasaki* (Stackpole Books, 1995)
Francillon, René J., *Japanese Aircraft of the Pacific War* (Putnam, 1970)
Freeman, Roger A., *Camouflage & Markings – United States Army Air Force* (Ducimus Books, 1974)
Herbert, Kevin, *Maximum Effort – The B-29s Against Japan* (Sunflower University Press, 1983)

Howlett, Chris, *Boeing B-29 Superfortress Owners' Workshop Manual* (Haynes Publishing, 2015)

Link, Mae Mills and Hurbert, Coleman, *Medical Support of the Army Air Forces in World War II* (Office of the Surgeon General, USAF, 1955)

Maguire, Jon A., *Gear Up! Flight Clothing & Equipment of USAAF Airmen in World War II* (Schiffer Military/Aviation History, 1995)

Mann, Robert A., *The B-29 Superfortress* (McFarland & Company, Inc Publishers, 2004)

Marshall, Chester, *B-29 Photo Combat Diary – The Superfortress in World War II and Korea* (Specialty Press Publishers and Wholesalers, 1996)

Millman, Nicholas, *Osprey Aircraft of the Aces 100 – Ki-44 'Tojo' Aces of World War 2* (Osprey Publishing, 2011)

Nijboer, Donald, *Cockpit – An Illustrated History of World War II Aircraft Interiors* (Boston Mills Press, 1998)

Nijboer, Donald, *Gunner – An Illustrated History of World War II Aircraft Turrets and Gun Positions* (Boston Mills Press, 2001)

Nijboer, Donald, *Graphic War – The Secret Aviation Drawings and Illustrations of World War II* (Firefly Books, 2005)

Ross, Stewart Halsey, *Strategic Bombing by the United States in World War II* (McFarland & Company, Inc Publishers, 2003)

Sakai, Saburo, *Samurai* (Ballantine Books, 1958)

Sakaida, Henry, *Osprey Aircraft of the Aces 22 – Imperial Japanese Navy Aces 1937–45* (Osprey Publishing, 1998)

Sakaida, Henry, *Osprey Aircraft of the Aces 13 – Japanese Army Air Force Aces 1937–45* (Osprey Publishing, 1997)

Takaki, Koji and Sakaida, Henry, *Osprey Aviation Elite Units 5 – B-29 Hunters of the JAAF* (Osprey Publishing, 2001)

Tillman, Barrett, *Whirlwind – the Air War Against Japan 1942–1945* (Simon & Schuster, 2010)

WEBSITES

www.40thbombgroup.org
www.346bg.com
www.B-29.org
www.444thbg.org
www.315bw.org

INDEX

Page numbers in **bold** refer to illustrations and their captions.

A6M2 Zero.sen 5, 17, 41, 76
air sea rescue 28, 73
air-to-air ramming 7, 45, 56, **56**, 59, **59**, 63, 69, 72
Akeno Army Flying School 5
Akeno Training Air Division **48**, 70
Allen, Edmund T. 11–12
American Volunteer Group (AVG) 35
armament
  B.29 Superfortress 4, 5, 6, **11**, 13, 15, **24**, 25, **25**, **27**, 44–45, 66
  Browning M.2 0.50.cal 5, **11**, 13, **24**, 25, **25**, **27**, 29, 40
  Ho.103 Type 1 12.7mm machine guns 5, 6, 19, 20, **20**, 21, 29, **30**, 31, 31–32, **31**, **32**
  Ho.301 40mm cannon 21, **32**
  Nakajima Ki.44 5, 6, 19, 20, **20**, 21, 28–29, 29, **30**, 31, 31–32, **32**, 67
  Type 89 7.7mm machine guns 5, 6, 19, 29, **30**, 31, **32**
Arnold, Gen H. H. "Hap" 15
atomic weapons 16, 28, 75
Avery, Lt Lloyd **61**, **64–66**

B.29 Superfortress
  42.6234 56
  42.6242 *Esso Express* **11**
  42.6274 *Lady Hamilton* 7, 55
  42.6299 *"humpin honey"* 56, **56**
  42.6330 54–55
  42.6360 56
  42.24494 *MARY ANN* **4**
  42.24623 *THUMPER* **62**
  42.65246 *Irish Lassie* **60**, **61**, **64–66**
  42.24464 *Flying Stud II* **36**
  42.24622 **55**
  42.24784 *Slick's Chicks* 51
  42.24815 *Deaner Boy* 51
  42.24856 *GOIN' JESSIE* **14**
  42.63315 *Bella Bortion* 56
  42.63363 *Marietta Misfit* 50
  42.65296 *The Ancient Mariner* **69**
  42.93852 *TOKYO ROSE* **58**, **59**
  44.27297 *BOCKSCAR* 75
  44.70072 *Limber Richard* **38**
  44.86292 *ENOLA GAY* 75
  armament 4, 5, 6, **11**, 13, 15, **24**, 25, **25**, **27**, 44–45, 66
  bomb-bays 4, 10, 16, 25, 28
  cockpit **42**
  crew 15, 24, **24**, **44**
  deployment 7, 15, 24, 35–36, 77
  design and development 6, 10–13, 15–16, 22, 24, 25–26
  engines 5, 6, 11–12, 22, **23**, 24, 26, **26**, 28, 61
  fields of fire **27**
  fire control system 5, 10, **12**, 13, **13**, 43–44, **44**, 52, 53, 61–62
  Korean War service 77, **77**
  performance 4, 22, 24–25, 52
  prototypes **5**, 6, 11–14, 23–24, **23**
  specifications 4, 5, 22–28
  turrets 6, 12–13, **12**, **13**, **25**, 52–53
B.29 Superfortress, *Silverplate* 16, 28, 77
B.29A Superfortress 25–26
B.29B Superfortress 15, 26–27, 45, 66
B.29C Superfortress 27, **58**
Boeing 11, **13**, 16
bombing accuracy 62–63
bombs **4**, **69**
Burma 46

Central Aircraft Manufacturing Company 35
China 17, **37**, 41, 44, 46, 50
China-Burma-India (CBI) Theater of Operations 15, 36, 46
chronology 8–9
Communist Chinese Air Force 76
computers 13
Consolidated 11

Doolittle, Lt Col James H. 35
Doty, Andy 6
Douglas 11

escort fighters 38, 52, 66, 68, 70
F.13 27
Far East Air Force 77

friendly fire 61–62

Germany, war with 11
Gilonski, Sgt Walter 54
Guam 35, **38**

Hanson, Maj Charles 54–55
Hawker Hurricane 16–17
Hiroshima 16, 75
Honda, Capt Kanji 70

Imperial Japanese Naval Air Force (IJNAF) 5, 36–37, 46, 71–72, 74
Imperial Japanese Navy 33
incendiary attacks 60–61, 62–63
India 36, 54–55
Ishikawa, Maj Kanshi **68**, 69
Iwo Jima **34**, 72

JAAF 5, 16–17, 29–30, 36–37, 49, 69–74
JAAF formations
  5th Hikoshidan 46
  9th Hiko Sentai 7, 55–56
  10th Air Division 70
  10th Hikoshidan 51
  11th Air Division 70
  23rd Hiko Sentai 68
  30th Air Fighter Group 70
  47th Dokuritsu Hiko Chutai 19–20
  47th Hiko Chutai 29–30
  47th Hiko Sentai **49**, **54**, 59, 60, **64–66**, 70, **70**
  64th Hiko Sentai, 54–55
  70th Hiko Sentai 51, 56, 59–60, 62–63, **63**, 68, 70, **70**, 74
  104th Hiko Sentai 56
  204th Hiko Sentai 54–55
  246th Hiko Sentai 31, 59–60, 68, **68**, 69, 70
  Flying Training Units 49
Japan 33, 35, 37–38, 38, 49, 69–70, 70, 71–72, 74
jet stream 53–54, **53**

Kawasaki Ki.60 **21**
Kawasaki Ki.61 20
Kawasemi Butai (Kingfisher Force) 19
Kennedy, Maj W. L. 40
Kobe raid 68–69
Kofukada, Lt Cdr Mitsugu 55
Koku Hombu 7, 19, 20
Kokusai Ki.86a 45
Kono, Capt Kensui 74
Korean War 77, **77**
Koyama, Yasushi 7
Kurai, 2Lt Toshio 51

Lanahan, Sgt Harold 54
LeMay, Maj Gen Curtiss 15, 26, 44–45, 62, 63
Lockheed 11
Luftwaffe 21

Makasan railway depot raid 7
Manchuria Airplane Manufacturing Company 50, 56
Mariana Island archipelago **34**, 36, 38, 58, 72–73
mercy sorties 75–76
Miyabe, Capt Hideo 54–55
Morgan, Lt Col Bob **66**
Mori, Shigenobu 17
Mukden raid 73
Musashino raid **60**, **64–66**

Nagasaki 16, 75
Nakajima aircraft factory raid 66, 68
Nakajima Hikoki KK (Nakajima Aircraft Company) 17, 19, 20, 28
Nakajima Ki.12 17
Nakajima Ki.27 Nate 16, 17
Nakajima Ki.43 Oscar 5, 16, 17, 19, **49**, 54–55, 76
Nakajima Ki.44 Shoki 70, 74, **76**
  armament 5, 6, 19, 20, **20**, 21, 28–29, 29, **30**, 31, 31–32, **32**, 67
  cockpit 6, **32**, **47**
  deployment 37–38
  design and development 16–17, **17**, 19–21, **21**, 28–32
  engines 4, 6, 19, 20, 29, 31, 32
  evaluation trials 6–7, 19–20, **21**, 29–30

performance 6–7, 19, 29, 31, 58, 74
pre-production 29–30
production 5, 20, 21, 38, 76
specifications 28
Nakajima Ki.44-I 5, 30–31
Nakajima Ki.44-II 5, **7**, **8**, **18**, 20–21, **30**, 31–32, **31**, **32**, **37**, **47**, **48**, **60**, 70
Nakajima Ki.44-II Hei 31, 32, **54**, **63**, **75**
Nakajima Ki.44-II Otsu 21, 32, 68–69
Nakajima Ki.44-III 20–21, 32
Nakajima Ki.87 5
Nationalist Chinese (Kuomintang) 76, **76**
Nattrass, MSgt William **55**
Nomonhan Incident 17

Ogawa, WO Makoto **18**, 51, **51**, 62
Operation *Matterhorn* 36
Otonari, Capt Sadahiko 69

Pacific theater of war **34**
Pearl Harbor, Attack on 11, 35
Philippines, the **31**, 35
Potts, Ivan 68–69

Quinlan, John P. 50, **50**

RAF 40, 77
Red Air Force 17, 33
Roosevelt, Franklin D. 35

Shimizu, Capt Jun **59**
Shinten Seiku Tai 7
Showa steelworks raids 7, 55–56
Smith-Hutton, Lt Cdr Henri 35
Solomon islands 46
Steakley, Capt John D. **58**, **59**
Strategic Air Command 77
strategic bombing campaign 10, 15, 52–56, 72
strategic situation 33, 34, 35–38

Tachikawa Ki.9 **45**
Tachikawa Ki.55 **45**
Tachikawa Ki.94 5
tactics
  American **57**, 60–63, 66, 68–70
  Japanese **18**, 20, **43**, 51, 56, **57**, 58–60, **59**, 63, 67, **67**
Taguchi, MSgt Mamoru 56
Tibbets, Col Paul W. 15
Tokyo 27, 33, 35, 38, 44–45, 51, 62–63
training 15, 39–41, **40**, **41**, 43–45, **43**, **44**, 45–46, **45**, 48–49, **48**, **49**, 66
transoceanic combat missions 72–73

US Bombing Survey 71, **71**
US Marine Corps 38, 72
US Navy 33, 35, 38
USAAC 10, 39–40, 49
USAAF 35–36
  3rd Photographic Reconnaissance Squadron 27
  VII Fighter Command 68, 72
  Eighth Air Force 52, 72
  9th BG **14**, **38**
  Twentieth Air Force 44, 75–76
  19th BG 6, **77**
  XX Bomber Command 36, 55–56, 61–62, 66, 72
  XXI Bomber Command 27, 38, 60–61, 62, 66, 68
  40th BG 7, 68–69
  58th BW 15, 24, 36
  73rd BW **62**, 66, 68
  315th BW 27, 45, 66
  444th BG **36**, 54–55, 56
  462nd BG 56
  468th BG **4**, 55
  497th BG **64–66**
  509th CG 77
Wagner, Lt Sam **55**
Wakamatsu, Yukiyoshi **37**
Westover, Maj Gen Oscar 11
winds 7, 53–54, **53**

Yoshida, Capt Yoshio 63, **63**, **73**, 74
Yoshioka, Yoshitaro **76**
Yuki, Sgt Masami **59**